Adopted in Love

ADOPTED IN LOVE

Contemporary Studies in Romans

Burton H. Throckmorton, Jr.

A Crossroad Book
THE SEABURY PRESS · NEW YORK

For Hamilton and Timothy

"...because I hold you in such affection..."

–PHILIPPIANS 1:7

1978

The Seabury Press
815 Second Avenue
New York, N.Y. 10017

Printed in the United States of America

Library of Congress Cataloging in Publication Data

Throckmorton, Burton Hamilton, 1921–
  Adopted in love.
  "A Crossroad book."
  1. Bible. N.T. Romans—Criticism, interpretation etc.   I. Title.
BS2665.2.T48   227'.1'06   77–22143   ISBN 0–8164–1230-8

Contents

Preface   vii

1. Revealing God's Righteousness   1
2. Righteousness and Wrath   11
3. Ransomed by Grace   18
4. Hope Based on Love   28
5. Adam and Sin   37
6. In Adam or in Christ?   46
7. Dead to Sin and Alive to God   53
8. The Power of Sin Versus the Freedom of Human Beings   62
9. Adopted in Love   72
10. Are Jews Also to be Saved?   79
11. Only One Commandment   88
12. Free to Love, but Not Free Not to Love   98
13. The Body of Christ Is One   107

Preface

THE BIBLE is highly prized by many but not well understood even in the church. We know, in general, why the Bible is prized, but why do many who cherish it know so inadequately and only indirectly what it actually says? The reasons, I think, are fairly clear. In the first place, the Bible is *not* an easy book to read or to understand. Many well-educated and intelligent Christians simply cannot understand much of it, and they are sometimes embarrassed to admit the fact because of a widespread but naïve assumption that *everyone* should be able to understand it. The situation is, however, that the Bible is not self-explanatory, that it comes from a very different time and place from ours, and that assistance is required if it is to be understood in a way that is significant for our lives. The reader needs light, guidance, and elucidation.

But where is one to go for the guidance one needs?

Christians who have had a theological education may read commentaries on the various biblical books, but for a number of reasons many lay people do not find commentaries very enticing, even if they are available. The commentary involves a format too academic in appearance for some people. It is, perhaps, overmuch a study book, which smacks of the classroom, to be read a bit at a time, and never straight through. Furthermore, most of the best commentaries are written primarily for theological students and biblical scholars and are consequently not particularly illuminating to the average churchgoer.

This little book is neither a commentary nor an expanded translation. Nor is it designed to be a substitute for commentaries. Its purpose is to offer the lay person the possibility of studying Paul's letter to the Romans on a precommentary level and apart from the commentary method.

The text of Romans is not interpreted word by word or even verse by verse. I have attempted, rather, to articulate in clear but adequate language some of the *major* ideas with which Paul is concerned in his letter to the church at Rome. I have tried to represent accurately the thought of Romans, without, on the one hand, pretending to represent the whole range of that thought, and without, on the other hand, so simplifying Paul as to misrepresent him. I have clearly tried to walk a fairly fine line, endeavoring to avoid both the complexities of full exposition and the falsification of oversimplicity.

The book follows the order of Paul's letter, the section of Romans to be discussed in each chapter being indicated at the beginning of the chapter. Throughout the book the ideas in Romans are discussed in sequence. This is not a *systematic* treatment either of Paul's thought as a whole or of the thought of Romans. It is to be hoped that Romans will be read along with this book, or, perhaps, before and after the reading of this book, and that the book will be used to shed light on Romans and not vice versa.

The theological significance of Romans is, of course, unsurpassed by any Christian writing. But as it stands it is too complex, too tightly knit, and is too ancient a writing for the Christian without a good deal of theological training to grasp; and commentaries on it tend only to highlight its complexity. On initial study of the letter, the lay person ought not be forced to confront all the intricacies, the turns of thought, and the theologically significant allusions and presuppositions that it contains. Nor should one be required to work through a detailed analysis of the whole text. Books should be made available that are true to the biblical text but that go at the lay person's pace. To this end I submit this book to the lay person, with the hope of clarifying some of the thought of Romans, without compromising the intention of the great apostle.

It should be noted that this book is a rewritten form of my earlier little work, *Romans for the Layman*. As even the title indicates, the language of that book was flagrantly sexist, though at the time I was naïvely unaware of the fact. In this work, written for women and about women, as much as for and about men, I have mortally wounded all references to "man," "men," "mankind," "fellow man," "brother," "brethren," and "son of God," as well as practically every masculine pronoun ("he," "his," "him," "himself" used—as it is euphemistically put—"generically"). But the sexist structure of English vocabulary still plagues us. "Sonship," for example, is a male term, with no female counterpart, let alone a word that will do for both sexes. The word, therefore, appears occasionally in the discussion of Rom. 8.

But it is not only the sexist language of this book that has been altered. Since *Romans for the Layman* appeared, my interpretation of Romans 6 and 7 has undergone some radical changes; I have therefore completely rewritten the material on those chapters, as well as the discussion of sacrifice in chap. 3.

Finally, I want to record here my gratitude to twenty-three classes of students at Bangor Seminary, with whom I have studied Romans during twelve semesters. Far more than they will ever know, and in ways most of them will probably never understand, they have taken me through Paul's letter as I have taken them. Or, said better: we have led each other in a mutual quest for illumination of historical existence whose mysteries always remain ultimately unpenetrated.

BURTON H. THROCKMORTON, JR.

Bangor Theological Seminary

CHAPTER I

Revealing God's Righteousness

ROM. I:I-I7

PAUL introduces himself to the church in the capital of the Roman Empire. He is a slave of Christ Jesus, called to be an apostle, set apart to preach the gospel. He is not his own master but a subject of Christ, summoned to be sent out, chosen to obey the command to preach. He has his orders from his Master: he must preach Jesus Christ, the Lord of the church. He must explain and elaborate the action God has just taken in his Son to restore broken lives to wholeness and to create a new community in Christ of people reconciled to one another and to God.

Paul's mission is primarily to Gentiles, that is, to non-Jews, to those many men and women, the great majority of humankind, whom the Jews from early days had held to be outside the sphere of God's revealing and redeeming work. Among these Gentiles who have never known the promises of God but who are nonetheless heirs of his promises are,

I

of course, the Romans. A small church has been founded among them, but Paul has never visited it, and he yearns to strengthen and encourage it, to preach the gospel there as he had so often planned to do. For the gospel is God's saving power—saving for *everyone* who will accept it, whether Jew or Greek. To preach the gospel is to make available to anyone who will appropriate it the saving power of Almighty God. Paul does not doubt this, for he has himself received the faith that he had once tried to destroy. The preacher, the one who is called and appointed to be a slave, is the frail but indispensable mediator of the power of God that alone can save. In the gospel that Paul preaches, God's righteousness is being revealed, but not apart from faith. We must now try to understand what this last statement means.

What does it mean to speak of "the revealing of God's righteousness"? What does Paul mean by righteousness? We must first inquire about what righteousness meant in the Judaism from which Paul came.

For the Hebrew every act of God was a righteous act. What God did was "righteous" simply because it was God who had done it. And there could be no righteousness anywhere that was different from God's righteousness. In other words, for the Jew there could be only one standard of righteousness, the same everywhere: it always and in every place corresponded to the will and judgments and acts of God.

Who, then, was the righteous *person?* The righteous person was the one whose action corresponded to the will of God, who is righteous—the one whom, therefore, the righteous God vindicated, delivered, "justified," or saved. The righteous person was the person whom God would bless, either in this life or in the life to come. On the other hand, the unrighteous person was the person whose action did not correspond to the will of God, whom God did *not* vindicate, deliver, "justify," or save. The unrighteous person could not expect to receive the blessing of God. Hence, to be righteous connoted both an accomplishment of man or woman, and a deed of God. Let us look at these two connotations separately, beginning with the latter.

To "have righteousness" or to "be righteous" was to be delivered by God from sin and death, to be open to receive God's blessing in this age or in the age to come. Righteousness, in this sense, meant deliverance or salvation. Compare, for example, the words of Isa. 51:5:

> My *righteousness* draws near speedily,
> my *salvation* has gone forth.

The terms "righteousness" and "salvation" are used as synonyms; hence the RSV translates the former word as "deliverance." The word that Isaiah used means righteousness, but he used it in the sense of deliverance. Similarly, the oft-memorized Ps. 24 uses the word "righteousness" in the same sense:

> Who shall ascend into the hill of the Lord?
> Or who shall stand in his holy place?
> He that hath clean hands, and a pure heart;
> Who hath not lifted up his soul unto vanity,
> Nor sworn deceitfully.
> He shall receive the blessing from the Lord,
> And *righteousness* from the God of his salvation.

Here again "righteousness" means deliverance or salvation: he who has clean hands and a pure heart shall receive blessing and *salvation,* literally, "righteousness," from God, who alone can save. Salvation is deliverance from sin and from death, and reconciliation with one's neighbor is reconciliation with God.

Sometimes in the Old Testament, then, righteousness equals salvation. The emphasis of the word is on a redeeming act of God. The one who is given righteousness is the one who is saved by God. But if one had asked a Hebrew what criterion God used in determining whom he would deliver, "make righteous," the Hebrew would usually have answered that God delivered the person whose actions corresponded to his will as recorded in the Scriptures. The one whom God saved was the one who obeyed God's law, the one who had "clean hands, and a pure heart." Hence, righteousness also meant godliness—obedience to the revealed will of God. This meaning of the word "righteousness" pervades the Old Testament and is the meaning that most of us no doubt commonly associate with the word: the righteous person is the person *worthy* of salvation. According to this view, the one whom God "makes righteous" is the one who, at least to some degree, is already righteous, the deed of God vindicating the performance of the human being. Righteousness to the Jew, as Paul understood Judaism, was *earned* righteousness: to be righteous was to have obeyed and merited a reward.

With this Jewish understanding of righteousness in mind, let us now turn to consider what Paul means by the word "righteousness." We shall immediately see both a similarity and a difference. Paul, like his fellow Jews, closely associates righteousness with salvation, but he differs from Judaism in the way in which he understands righteousness to be had. For the Jew, as we have seen, righteousness was to be earned, at least in part, by obeying the law, while for Paul righteousness could not be earned at all but could be received only as a gift of God and only by faith. Paul's formula is: righteousness by faith and not by works. We usually speak of *"justification* by faith," but the two English words "justification" (derived from Latin) and "righteousness" (derived from Anglo-Saxon) translate one Greek word used by Paul, and we shall here consistently use the latter word, "righteousness."

Paul, under the influence of the Old Testament, also understands righteousness both in an ethical sense and as a deed of God, but his emphasis, unlike that of the Old Testament, is on the latter. Let us refer to righteousness understood as a deed of God as "forensic" righteousness, in distinction from "ethical" righteousness. Paul sometimes uses the word "righteousness" to refer only or primarily to ethical behavior when dealing with the ethical life of *non-Christians,* but if one should ask whether Paul ever means "good deeds" when he refers to the righteousness of *Christians,* the answer would have to be both yes and no. The answer would be yes if one thought of this righteousness as a gift of God, but it would be no if one thought of it as a "work," that is, as something earned by one's performance under law. In other words, righteousness for Paul does have an ethical connotation when applied to Christians, but it is entirely divorced from any notion of merit. The "fruit of righteousness" that ought to characterize a Christian's life is not the Christian's own doing but is "through Jesus Christ" (cf. Phil. 1:11).

Now we must acknowledge that it is very difficult for us to think about ethical behavior totally apart from any overtones of merit. This is not so much because we are Jews at heart as it is because of our puritanical heritage. We say to ourselves that the word "righteous" implies a norm or standard, and that adhering to a norm or measuring up to a standard implies accomplishment. The righteous person is therefore the ethical person, the one who has succeeded in his or her ethical performance. Hence the ethical person is also the person who has earned a reward for success in obeying. The person who is righteous in an ethical sense is thought to be the person who has earned something for himself, or herself—namely, the reward of salvation from God, who is righteous. We may not always articulate our thinking as carefully as this, but is this not the assumption under which we commonly live?

If, however, this be our assumption with regard to the meaning and end of righteousness, we confront a great difficulty when we read Paul. For Paul denies categorically that the righteous Christian has *earned* anything before God by his or her righteousness. He does not deny that righteousness has an ethical aspect. What he does deny is that ethical righteousness *merits* the believer one whit before God. Why he makes this denial will soon become clear.

Let us look now at the other sense in which Paul uses the word "righteousness"—the forensic sense, which he emphasizes over the ethical sense. When used forensically, righteousness describes not primarily an ethical quality but a *relationship*. As so used, righteousness is understood not as a possession that one has earned and that one can bring before God but as a *verdict* pronounced by God. ("Forensic" is derived from the Latin word *forum,* the public place in each city where, among other things, courts of justice were held.) The verdict, "You are righteous," means, "You are acquitted." In relation to the court the one "acquitted" or "made righteous" is not guilty. The court's verdict *may* correspond to the defendant's performance, and it may not, but the decisive factor that determines the destiny of the defendant's life in the community is not his or her performance but the verdict pronounced in the forum. If the verdict is "guilty," the defendant may be imprisoned or even executed, whether or not he committed the crime of which he was accused; and, contrariwise, if the verdict is "not guilty," the defendant's life in the community will be unaltered whether or not he committed the crime of which he was accused. Let us repeat: the decisive factor in a person's life is the verdict under which he or she stands, quite aside, it may be, from performance.

When, then, Paul uses the word "righteous" ("righteousness") in a forensic sense, he refers to God's acquittal, his verdict, "Not guilty." The one who has received righteousness is the one who has received acquittal at God's bar of justice. When *God's* judgment is involved, however, the acquitted one is to be thought of as *really* righteous, and not simply as one who is *regarded* as righteous when in fact he is not. The distinction sometimes made between what one is and what one is regarded to be is not legitimate when it is God who does the regarding. What God regards one to be is what one is and not what one thinks oneself to be or what another thinks one to be. Conversely, be it also noted that it is only because God *regards* one as a sinner that one *is* a sinner. If, therefore, God declares one to be righteous, one *is* righteous in the only important sense of what it means to be righteous, in the only sense that is decisive for one's life and destiny.

For Paul, then, the righteous person is the person whom God declares to be and accepts as righteous. Righteousness thus becomes a possibility only in relation to God. The primary focus of the word is not on one's performance but on one's relationship to God. When Paul speaks of a believer as righteous, his emphasis is not on the believer's behavior but on the believer's orientation, not on *what* the believer has done but on the fact that what he or she has done—whatever it may be—has grown out of and has been determined by his or her relation to God in Christ. On what ground, according to Paul, is one made righteous by God if not by obeying the law? Paul's answer is that one is made righteous *by faith.* The ground of righteousness is not obedience to the law but faith. We must now try to understand what Paul means by the word "faith."

Paul sometimes uses "faith" in two characteristically Jewish senses: *(a)* as meaning faithfulness and reliability, or *(b)* as meaning trust, belief, or confidence. But far more often the word has more specifically Pauline connotations. We may mention three of these:

In the first place, faith, as we have seen, is closely related to righteousness in the forensic sense. Faith is openness to the reception of God's righteousness. It therefore presupposes humility and the acknowledgment of guilt, that is, the acknowledgment that one has sinned. One does not accept acquittal from God unless one believes one needs to be acquitted, unless one bears the burden of guilt. It is faith, for Paul, and not obedience to the law that makes righteousness possible.

In the second place, righteousness in an ethical sense is

possible only in faith. For Paul, it is only the act done in *faith* that is not sinful, for an act done in faith is not done for reward but is done in gratitude, gratitude to God for the life he has offered in Jesus Christ. Hence faith is closely related to gratitude as well as to righteousness, for gratitude must follow from faith's reception of righteousness.

In the third place, the attitude of faith precludes the attitude of boasting. By boasting Paul does not mean simply verbal bragging: he refers to the inner attitude that assumes one is meriting something before God. It is precisely because any ethical behavior that grows out of obedience to the law gives grounds for boasting that such behavior is for Paul always sin. A distinction is made between the compulsion of law and the compulsion of love. If I keep a law, rather than break it, I merit a reward under the law, and deserve to be distinguished from others who have broken it. But if I do a deed because *love* compels it, I do not merit anything, nor do I desire to. And should the one on whose behalf I acted in love "reward" me, I should be offended, for I would know that my act had not been interpreted as truly an act of love. It is not the character of love either to merit or to seek reward. The only reciprocation love desires is love. Faith, then, is closely related not only to righteousness and gratitude but also to love. Boasting separates; love unites. The action that faith takes is an act in love. Love is faith at work, the faith that has received God's acquittal in Christ exerting itself.

Perhaps the relation between forensic and ethical righteousness can now be seen more clearly. In both senses of the word, righteousness is had in a relationship with God. In its forensic sense righteousness refers to God's acquittal; in its ethical sense righteousness refers to an action done by a believer under the condition of acquittal. For Paul, to describe a Christian as ethically righteous is not to say that he or she has acted in obedience to a law but rather that he or she has acted in love out of gratitude for acquittal. It is not, then, *what* a believer has done that makes him righteous in an ethical sense but *why* he has done it.

And so Paul writes to the Romans that the righteousness of God is being revealed, that is to say, is being offered now to anyone who will accept it in faith.

For Further Thought . . .

1. Do we ordinarily think of righteousness in Jewish terms, or in Paul's terms?
2. Do we perform righteous acts primarily for reward?
3. Discuss the view that Paul's understanding of righteousness frees one to be righteous.
4. Are we free to do what we think is right, or do the opinions of others hinder us? If they do, is this right or wrong?
5. Is it true in your own personal life that more time is spent on reflection on your obedience than on your disobedience?
6. Discuss what Paul means by the quotation he uses in Rom. 1:7 from Hab. 2:4: "He who through faith is righteous shall live." Would Paul agree that it is possible for a person to be righteous in any way other than "by faith"?

CHAPTER 2

Righteousness and Wrath

PAUL has said that God is now offering acquittal, through Jesus Christ, to all people who will receive it by faith. But the question arises: Which ones need acquittal? Or, to put the question differently, To whom is the gospel relevant? Paul's answer is quite clear: both Gentiles and Jews—that is, all people—stand in need of appropriating the righteousness that is from God and that is receivable by faith.

Paul explains the need of the Gentiles first. As he has pointed out that in the gospel the *righteousness* of God is being revealed to faith, so he now points out that the *wrath* of God is being revealed where there is *not* faith. Paul is not of the opinion that in ancient times God's wrath was revealed and that in the present time God is disclosing his righteousness. No, God's wrath accompanies his righteousness in the present time: the two go together. The time of acquittal is also the time of condemnation. In short, Paul believes that the last days are at hand, the days when both righteousness and wrath are manifested. These two words, then, "righteousness" and "wrath," are, to use a long but indispensable theological term, "eschatological." This means that they refer to what is expected to take place at the end of the present historical age. (The Greek word *eschata* means "last things." The English adjective based on this word is eschatological, meaning pertaining to the last things—the last days, when this historical age will come to its close, when the judgment will be performed and God's kingdom will be established.)

When Paul speaks of the wrath of God as being revealed, we must not understand him to mean that *hate* is being revealed. Wrath is not hate. Hate opposes love; wrath is the form love takes with those who oppose it. Hate is unjust; wrath is just. Hate seeks to destroy; wrath forgives. So when Paul says that the wrath of God is being disclosed along with his righteousness, he is saying that God is offering acquittal but that those who refuse to accept it are condemned.

God's wrath and condemnation is falling upon godless and unrighteous people, who have known God but have neither glorified him nor been grateful to him. Paul is thinking primarily of the Gentiles, of the multitudes outside of Israel, who have not known the law that was given through Moses, to be sure, but who nevertheless have always been able to know *something* about God through nature. There has never been anyone born whom God has totally prevented from knowing anything about him. One need only perceive the world that God has created to know God's power and divinity. But the Gentiles have not turned to the

Creator of the world; they have turned instead to the world he has created and looked to created things for their salvation. In short, the Gentiles are guilty of idolatry. Why is idolatry sin? Because it looks to weakness for strength; it looks to the perishing for life; it looks to a created thing or to a creature, to an institution or to some human enterprise, for the salvation that only God can give. Idolatry is the ultimate misjudgment that ultimately destroys.

The Gentiles were worshiping, as most people did, but they were not worshiping God. Therefore, God gave them up: he handed them over to perish with the images to which they clung. The righteousness of God became wrath against unrighteousness. The Gentiles had become immoral, degrading their bodies. Paul specifies their sin, listing first their sexual sins and then their social sins, in accordance with a common division of sins into two types. The Gentiles were not only practicing these sins; they were also sympathizing with those who practiced them. They knew God's command, but they neither obeyed it nor encouraged others to do so. They were therefore deserving of death.

So Paul analyzes the state of the Gentiles. But what about the Jews? The Jews, having and knowing the commands of God, stood in judgment of the Gentiles. They were horrified by pagan immorality. But the important question was not what the Jews *knew,* but what they *did,* and Paul did not find them innocent of the charges they were bringing against pagans. God judges the actions of a person, not his or her knowledge, and the standard by which he judges is the same for all people. According to this standard, Paul found the Jews to be as guilty as the Gentiles. Again and again Paul emphasizes the ultimate significance of what one *does.* The decisive question to be asked about the Jews was not, Do they have the law? or, Do they know God's will? The decisive question was, Do they practice day by day what they know to be the command of God? And if anyone asked this last question with regard to the Jews, the answer must be, No, they do not.

The Jews' understanding of themselves in relation to God was confused. Because they had the law by which God judges, and knew the contents of this law, they deceived themselves by not fully realizing and taking seriously the fact that they themselves must also be judged by the law that they possessed. It commonly occurs that when one has the standard by which judgment is made, one easily applies the standard to others and tends to identify one's possession of the standard with one's conformity to it. To have the norm leads to the delusion that one is immune to it, or exempt from it. This danger arises in a peculiar way to confront all religious people, and we must not think of the Jews as uniquely guilty in this respect. Knowing the canons of a faith, or standing in the heritage of a faith, the religious person distinguishes between himself and all those who stand outside the faith to which he adheres, and he assumes that some virtue inherently accrues to him because of his superior knowledge and lineage.

If one were to make a general statement about the ethical behavior of various peoples living in the first-century Mediterranean world, one might have to say that the Jews were superior, morally, to the pagans. No doubt Paul would have affirmed this had he been pressed into making this kind of judgment. But the moral superiority of the Jews led them to censure the less moral pagans without at the same time adequately censuring themselves. Hence Paul reminds the Jews that they will not escape the judgment of God, even though they be superior to other peoples. The question is not whether they are superior; the question is, as Paul sees it, whether they are totally obedient. And Paul asks the Jews whether they are taking too lightly the fact that God has been so good to them in the past and has shown them such forbearance and patience. They ought not presume upon God's great kindness, for it is not a rubber stamp on all their misdoings but is meant to lead them to repent. Because they have been stubborn and unrepentant, the Jews are storing up wrath for themselves for the final day of wrath, when God will disclose his righteous judgment, for God will give to each one in accordance with his or her performance.

It is very important for us to notice that Paul is quite clear in stating that it is by one's *works* that God judges one who does not accept righteousness by faith. There are only two states or conditions in which one may stand before God: one may either appear in faith in Jesus Christ and accept reconciliation through Christ, or one may appear outside of faith, rejecting God's gift and pointing instead to one's performance. God's judgment on those who reject the righteousness disclosed in Christ is based strictly on what they have done. If it should happen that someone fully obeyed the law, God would grant that person glory and honor and peace. But God will not grant reward to anyone who has not fully earned it, except under the condition he has offered in Christ. There is no partiality in God. And this is just the trouble! It is precisely because God shows no partiality, because it is his nature always to judge all people justly by the same standard, that he has acted to redeem humankind in an altogether new way in Jesus Christ. Now one need no longer appeal to one's own ambiguous righteousness; one may rather accept as a sheer gift from God, offered in Jesus Christ, a righteousness that, like any gift one may receive, both is and is not one's own.

The Jew, then, under the law, is judged strictly in accordance with his or her obedience to the law. One who appeals to the law must rest one's case exclusively on one's performance. Paul now makes a further point, namely, that one who appeals to one's performance under the law must be judged by one's performance in relation to *all* the laws and not simply in relation to the laws one has managed to keep. He reminds the Jews that in one's relation to any legal system one is guilty if one has broken a single law. A judge does not ask a person how many laws he has kept; if a man or woman has broken one law, he or she is guilty. And so Paul says that it is profitable to keep the circumcision law only if all the other laws have also been obeyed.

What is important, however, is not the external manifestation of correctness, but the inner, secret desire and predisposition to obey the moral law. No Jew could have granted Paul's assumption here that "ritual" laws—as, for example, the circumcision law—are less binding than "moral" laws, and Paul's statements on the subject are not so clear as they might be. Paul is here breaking new ground, and he will later be more explicit. But this point is clear: the Jew is guilty if he breaks a single law, no matter how many other laws he has faithfully obeyed.

For Further Thought . . .

1. Do you believe that God ever hates anyone, or do you believe that God only loves? What answer do you think Paul would give?

2. In Paul's view were the Jews, who obeyed God's commandments, in a more favorable position before God than the Gentiles were who did not obey the commandments? If not, what is the point of obeying God's commandments?

3. Discuss the reasons people have for not responding in faith to "the revealing of God's righteousness."

CHAPTER 3

Ransomed by Grace

PAUL's estimation of the situation of the Jews leads him to ask whether or not this elect people of God has any advantage over all other people. If, with respect to the law, the Jews were guilty, then what was the significance of the Jews' unique relationship with God, who had promised them life? Do the Jews still have an advantage? Paul answers that they have, and that their advantage is in their possession of the words of God. By the "words of God," Paul is referring in the first instance to the words of Scripture, which in the church make up the Old Testament. In the immediate context of Romans, however, the possession of these words of God does not seem to be an advantage, for it is precisely in relation to these words that the Jews are condemned. It is, then, only within the larger framework of the purposes of God that the Jews may be said to have an advantage in having the words that God has entrusted to them. By the words of God, then, Paul does not have in mind the *commands* of God contained in Scripture: possession of the commands has not turned out to be an advantage! Paul is rather thinking more specifically of the *promises* of God that are found in the Old Testament, the words that have been fulfilled in Christ. It is the Jews to whom these promises were initially made, and God will not go back on his promises, for *God* is faithful though every human being be unfaithful.

And so the Jews do have an advantage in that they have been entrusted with the promises made by God, who is faithful, but their advantage over other peoples is *not* due to any superiority, on their part, in ethical performance. All are under sin, both Jews and Greeks. This statement summarizes the main thrust of the first two chapters of Romans. "None is righteous, no, not one." Paul quotes from a number of psalms to substantiate his judgment. The law speaks to those under the law, and both Jews and Greeks stand under law. Therefore, no one from among either Jews or Greeks can successfully defend his or her performance, as everyone will be called upon to do at the time of the Last Judgment. On the basis of obedience to the law no one can be made righteous before God. The law cannot make anyone righteous; on the contrary, it is precisely because of the existence of the law and of the necessity to live under the law that one knows one is *not* righteous but is a sinner. Under the law one is condemned: the plight of the whole of humankind is that it stands under law, is guilty in relation to law, and is not able to alter its condition.

But, standing guilty and condemned under the law, one may now hear the gospel—the good news that condemnation is not inevitable, that freedom and life are now possible. God is offering humankind *righteousness.* His righteousness—the possibility of acquittal—is being made available to all who have faith. Acquittal, not possible under the law, is now being offered *apart from* and *around* the law. What both Jews and Gentiles have painfully discovered cannot be achieved in relation to law may now be had through faith in Jesus Christ (or, perhaps, through the faith *of* Jesus Christ). God is making righteousness available to *all.* He is not offering it only to one people, or to a select group of people. "All have sinned"; all "fall short of the glory of God"; all are in want; all are less than they might be and ought to be; and God is making no distinctions among any of his lost ones. In Jesus Christ he is making righteousness available to *anyone* who will receive it. This righteousness is *free!* It is given "for nothing," a sheer gift by the grace of God.

Perhaps we should now pause briefly to say a word about the meaning of "grace" in Paul's letters. "Grace," as Paul uses it, is a semitechnical word and requires some defining. When Paul speaks of the grace of God he does not mean primarily a quality of God, as, for example, the quality of kindness. By grace Paul means primarily an *act* of God, in Jesus Christ, on behalf of humankind. This act is a *gift.* The gift centers in the offering of Christ on the cross.

But, in the second place, grace is also revealed in Christ's offering of *himself* on the cross. The grace of God and the grace of Christ are the same grace: God's offering of Christ and Christ's offering of himself are the same offering—a gift made on Calvary on behalf of all who will receive it. And so the grace of God, the free gift of God in Christ, also reveals uniquely the *love* of God. Hence Paul can relate so closely the *grace* of the Lord Jesus Christ and the *love* of God. Both point the believer ultimately to the cross.

In the third place, we may note that in Paul's writings grace sometimes connotes *power*. When God's gift—or Christ's gift—of grace is received and appropriated, it manifests itself as a power that rules in those who receive it— a power opposed to, and ultimately victorious over, sin.

Having indulged in a brief digression in order better to understand what Paul means by grace, we shall pick up again the thread of Paul's thought in Romans. We have seen that the righteousness offered in Christ is a free gift to be had "for nothing." The gift may be *appropriated* for nothing: it is the giver who pays the price. One may be made righteous by the "grace of God" through the *ransoming* that takes place in Christ Jesus. What is meant by ransoming? To ransom is to buy back, to set free by the payment of a price. Paul understands salvation as a ransoming act, which, on the one hand, makes free and, on the other hand, pays a price. The Christian is a ransomed person, a person who has been bought back with a price. To redeem is to ransom (the two words have a common Latin root). One may be redeemed only if the price for one's redemption has been paid.

Having referred to God's ransoming act, Paul goes on to describe the price that was paid for the redemption that was made available. He states that God put forward Jesus Christ as an *expiation*. The Greek word Paul uses may also be translated "mercy seat" instead of "expiation." What would Paul have meant if he had said that God put forward Christ as a mercy seat? In Ex. 25:10–22 the mercy seat is described as a solid gold plate placed on top of the Ark in the tabernacle. In Lev. 16:11–17 the use of the mercy seat in connection with the Hebrews' ritual of atonement is explained. It may well be that Paul's intention was, at least in part, to allude to the mercy seat, on which blood was poured by the priest when the sin of Israel was being atoned for, but it is probably also true that Paul did not intend to limit his meaning to "mercy seat," for most Gentiles would probably not have known what the mercy seat was. Paul was surely also referring to Christ as an "expiation" for sin.

What is the meaning of expiation? To expiate is to make satisfaction for, to atone for. "Expiate" is also a translation for the Hebrew word "cover," used in connection with sin. Expiation should be distinguished from propitiation, which means to appease the wrath of an offended person or god. When, then, Paul says that God put forward Christ as an expiation, he means that God offered forgiveness in Christ, but he means also more than that. To put forward Christ on the cross as an expiation was to offer him as a *sacrifice.* That Paul understood the crucifixion as involving sacrifice is quite clear, for he refers to the expiation as "by his [i.e., Christ's] blood." The expiation for sin was a blood sacrifice.

What images were available for Paul to draw on by which to interpret Jesus' death as a blood sacrifice? In the first place, there was the Jewish sacrificial cult that was still being practiced in Paul's time in the temple in Jerusalem. The image here is of blood on the altar—offered to and received by God, thereby achieving the re-establishment of the covenant between God and the sacrificer: "It is the blood that makes atonement by reason of the life" (Lev. 17:11).

Sacrifice was the central act of external worship in Israel.

The Hebrews believed that when a sacrifice was made and the gift offered to God was accepted, union with God was achieved. The sacrifice was also believed to be a means of expiating sin. Of course, when the gifts were made they were partially or wholly destroyed, but the purpose of the destruction was not simply to destroy. The essence of sacrifice is not death or annihilation, as is sometimes held. God is not honored by the destruction of life. Death is not the essence of sacrifice; it is, properly speaking, no part of the sacrifice at all. The death of the animal, while it was a necessary preliminary to the sacrifice, was not a factor in the actual sacrifice, any more than the killing of an animal is a factor with us in the preparation of a stew for dinner. To "sacrifice" an animal is not to *kill* it. In fact, except in public sacrifices, it was not the priest who killed the animal; it was the sacrificer.

As has been indicated, the sacrifice provided a means of union with God. After God had accepted the victim that had been offered him, those who had made the offering ate what remained of the victim (what was not offered) in a religious meal, and so shared the sacrifice with God, strengthening the bond between them. But every sacrifice was also thought to have some *atoning* value. When a person sinned, he or she needed to find grace again, and had to ask God to re-establish the covenant whose terms he or she had broken. So the purpose of sacrifices for sin and sacrifices for expiation was to re-establish reconciliation.

But for Paul, of course, the blood that makes atonement is not *animal* blood. It is *human* blood—and not simply human blood, but the blood of the son of God. The idea of human sacrifice was always abhorrent to the Jews—

ghastly beyond description; and human blood was never offered on the altar in the temple of Jerusalem. Paul was groping for some image by which to interpret the meaning of the blood that was shed by Jesus on Calvary; and lying at hand for him, who had been a Jew, was the Jewish sacrificial cult. But, of course, there were differences.

In the case of Jesus, the victim is furnished by God himself, and not by men or women: *God* purposed (or, put forward) Christ Jesus as a blood expiation. Or, as Paul will say later in his letter: "God did not spare his own Son, but handed him over on behalf of us all" (Rom. 8:32; cf. 5:8). This blood expiation was not made *to* God, but *by* God, as the public way by which atonement is made possible. The sinner does not sacrifice to God; but God *gives* the life which men and women seek. This life is received when one identifies oneself with the blood of Christ "by faith." In the church the concept of sacrifice is turned on its axis: not man or woman who sacrifices in his or her own interest, but God who comes with the sacrifice who, metaphorically speaking, is his Son.

But in his interpretation of Jesus crucified—which was the center of his preaching—Paul may have drawn on images other than what was provided him by the temple cult in Jerusalem. Perhaps he was familiar with the view that the death of the Maccabean martyrs in the second century before Christ had atoning value. In IV Maccabees, Eleazar prays: "Let *our* punishment be a satisfaction on *their* behalf. Make *my blood their purification,* and take *my life* as a *ransom for theirs* (6:28f.). Like Paul in the case of Jesus' crucifixion, the author of IV Maccabees starts with the fact of particular human deaths, and asks what meaning can be wrested from the tragic fates of those martyrs. What *meaning?* No meaning at all? That is possible, but he offers an alternative to the supposition of meaninglessness: he presumes to declare that their death will benefit others. Perhaps Paul knew of the faith that the human blood of the Maccabean martyrs had atoning value for their successors.

Thirdly, Paul also may have been influenced by Jewish theology centering on the story referred to as the "Binding of Isaac," an expression that comes from Gen. 22:9. In rabbinic teaching the "Binding of Isaac" had atoning value. We find such statements as the following: "Reckon to *our* account the *Binding of Isaac* who was bound on the altar before Thee." And in another place Abraham prays: "I pray Thee, when the *descendants* of Isaac fall into sin and . . . no one intercedes for them, be Thou their Intercessor; may *his Binding* be remembered *in their favor,* and have mercy on them." It is possible that Paul was familiar with this "Binding of Isaac" theology, and it may have provided another image in his attempt to understand the meaning of the blood sacrifice of Christ. When Paul says: "God did not spare his own Son but gave him up for us all" (Rom. 8:32), the words "did not spare his own Son" are almost identical with the words God spoke to Abraham in Genesis: "Thou didst not spare thy son, thy only one" (Gen. 22:16).

The crucifixion of Christ was, for Paul, a blood sacrifice. Involving sacrifice, it shows that God is righteous, that his forbearance is not to be interpreted as indifference to sin. It also shows that God, through Christ, acquits the sinner. If, then, the sinner is acquitted by God while still a sinner, what happens to boasting? That is to say, if a guilty person is reconciled as a gift to the One against whom that person has done evil, how can such a guilty one make any appeal to his or her own virtue in the presence of the One who has freely forgiven? The answer is that he or she cannot. What Paul calls "boasting" is totally excluded by faith. It is not the case that a person in faith has never done any good works to which he or she may point; it is rather the case that a person in faith is oriented to God in a radically different way from a person who finds it necessary to appeal before God to his or her performance. A judgment one may pass on the relative goodness of one's works is based on orientation to law, to some standard in relation to which one may attempt to demonstrate one's virtue. But if one relinquishes one's orientation to law, one at the same time relinquishes the possibility of appealing to the standard by which alone one may measure the worth of one's performance.

If, then, one renounces the law by which one is condemned, one also at the same time renounces the law by which alone one is able to receive merit. One cannot have it both ways, discrediting the laws one fails to keep and honoring the laws one obeys. Paul emphasizes that the whole law stands or falls as a unit.

Hence the Christian, as delivered from the law, is delivered also from the possibility of boasting, of assuming superiority over anyone else before God. And it is precisely for this reason that one clings so tenaciously to the law, even though one is condemned by it, for only as the last possibility, only when no alternative way remains, will one let slip away the measuring rod by which one can point—for the benefit of oneself, of one's neighbors, and of God—to one's virtue.

For Further Thought . . .

1. What is the "grace" of God, and how is it related to the "grace" of Christ?
2. What are the implications of Paul's statement that, on Calvary, God put forward Christ? What part, then, did certain Jews and Pontius Pilate play in Jesus' crucifixion?
3. What is the relation of sin to law? Illustrate.
4. In Judaism sacrifices were means to establish union with God and to expiate sin. Can the sacrifice of Christ on the cross function in these two ways for the Christian? Does the Lord's Supper, or Holy Communion, help in answering this question? Explain.
5. Does it ever happen on the human level that the suffering or death of one person has reconciling value for others? Reflect on your own experience or observation in this regard.
6. Discuss the view that to give up "righteousness under law" for "righteousness by faith" is to give up one's security before God. Are people willing to give up this security for life in Christ? Why?

CHAPTER 4

Hope Based on Love

PAUL decided that he would clinch his argument—that a person can be made righteous only by faith and not by works—by citing the patriarch Abraham as an example of righteousness received on the ground of faith. So Paul took the Jews' most illustrious example of one who had *obeyed* God and showed that Scripture itself indicated that not even Abraham was made righteous on the basis of his works but that he also was righteous on the basis of faith. If it could be shown that Abraham had been made righteous by his works, this would have been an exception to Paul's statement that one can not be made righteous by works, and if there had been one exception, then presumably there could also be others. If, on the other hand, Paul could show that even Abraham had been made righteous not by works but by faith, then the possibility of anyone else's being made righteous by works would be practically eliminated.

Paul went to Gen. 15:6 for his proof text. There it was written in his Greek translation of Genesis: "Abraham believed [had faith in] God, and it was reckoned to him as righteousness." The passage does not say, "Abraham *obeyed* God and *earned* righteousness." Paul capitalizes on the word "reckoned," pointing out that wages that are earned are not reckoned to a worker but are his due. But Abraham had righteousness reckoned to him: he had not earned it by his performance.

Paul further points out that according to Genesis Abraham was not circumcised until *after* righteousness had been reckoned to him. And if Abraham was made righteous before he had been circumcised, then clearly his righteousness was not based on his conformity to the requirements of the law. Paul quotes Gen. 17:11, which says that Abraham's circumcision was a *sign,* and he interprets the sign as a seal or confirmation of the righteousness that had already been given to Abraham through his faith, even before he was circumcised. Thus Abraham, the great patriarch, is interpreted by Paul, not as the father of the circumcised, i.e., the Jews, for his circumcision had served simply to seal a prior event, but as the father of all those who are made righteous *by faith.* He becomes the patriarch of the New Israel, the church. The heirs of the promise made to Abraham are thus the Christians—those who do not earn righteousness but to whom righteousness is "reckoned" or attributed.

Before he leaves Abraham as his illustration *par excellence* of one who was made righteous by faith, Paul cites one of the most notable examples of Abraham's faith. Though Abraham was about a hundred years old, though his body was "as good as dead" and the womb of his wife Sarah was barren, yet Abraham did not waver in his faith in God's promise of offspring, being thoroughly convinced that God was able to do what he had promised. In this case also his faith was "reckoned" to him as righteousness, as the faith of those who are Abraham's spiritual descendants is also reckoned to them as righteousness.

Romans 5:1–11 may be viewed as a bridge between chaps. 1 to 4 and chaps. 5:12 to 8:39. The first four chapters are largely a theological analysis of the plight of humankind and of the saving action that God has taken in Jesus Christ. Chapters 5:12 to 8:39 is an analysis of life as renewed in Jesus Christ. In between is what may be thought of as a linking section, summing up what has preceded and anticipating what is to follow.

Paul begins by assuming a point that he has made before, namely, that we who believe have already been made righteous by faith, and he concludes from this assumption that we therefore have peace with God through our Lord Jesus Christ. Christians, as Christians, are already made righteous. To be made righteous by faith is, as we have seen, to be in a new relationship with God. The question then arises: In what kind of life does this new relationship issue? Paul is now to develop his answer to this question.

He says, in the first place, that those who are made righteous by faith have *peace* with God. Before God acted in Christ we were estranged from him; now we may have peace with him. God has made the peace, and so we are reconciled.

"Peace" is an eschatological word in the New Testament. It describes a relationship characteristic of life in the king-

dom, of life as fulfilled. It is not often used to describe one's
relationship to God, and when it is so used, it is used proleptically, describing as a present reality what is possible only
in anticipation. In the New Testament the peace that is said
to be had between a person and God is not, as it was among
the rabbis, a relationship established primarily by *the person;*
it is rather a relationship into which the believer is placed
by God. Peace is possible only if God *gives* it. It cannot be
earned or achieved by one's efforts, just as righteousness
cannot be earned but must be given by God.

So God in Christ has offered us peace. The gospel is the
good news that peace is now possible through Jesus Christ.
Thus it may be seen that peace is often synonymous with
salvation, and the "God of peace" is not the God who is
peaceful, or the God who brings peacefulness, but the God
who secures peace by overcoming the powers of evil
through his Messiah. Peace is a messianic, eschatological
word referring to a gift of God for which a high price has
been paid.

When, then, Paul writes that having been made righteous
by faith we have peace with God, he refers to the relationship with God into which the believer is put by grace—a
relationship of reconciliation. This relationship is made
available to the believer *at the present time,* and has become
a possibility particularly through the crucifixion of our Lord
Jesus Christ, for it is through Christ that we have been given
access to the reconciliation that we now enjoy.

Having described by the eschatological word "peace"
the life that is now a possible historical reality for believers,
Paul then characteristically uses another eschatological
word to distinguish between the "salvation" that is *now*

offered proleptically and the culmination of "salvation" that
remains a hope for the future. For Paul, the Christian life
is always in tension between the gift that one has received
and the gift for which one hopes. In the sixth chapter of
Romans this tension is elaborated. Here Paul distinguishes
between peace that one has and the glory of God for which
one still hopes. His purpose is not to lessen the significance
of the peace that has been given but to emphasize the glory
of the consummation that is so near and that Christians have
such good grounds for expecting. Christians indeed may
boast, not of what they have achieved, but of the fulfillment
of life that God is about to bestow on them, for which they
now hope.

How does one arrive at the place where one may hope?
Many people cannot hope. They have no grounds for hop-
ing, no reason for believing in the possibility of the fulfillment of hope. It is important, therefore, for us to note that
Paul describes antecedents to hope. Hope cannot be initiated by an act of the will; it cannot be assumed when there
are no grounds on which to base it. Before one can hope
with any degree of expectation that what one hopes for will
come to pass—and hope always presupposes some degree
of expectation—one must meet certain preliminary requirements. Paul now lists them.

We begin with suffering. It had been pointed out before
Paul that suffering born as chastisement can issue in good.
Suffering, says Paul, produces endurance. If one accepts
suffering, one learns to endure in the process. And endurance, in turn, produces what we may call "triedness" or
"proven-ness," an inner strength that has been hammered
out under the impact of trials and testings. And *then* one

may hope; then hope is justified; then that for which one hopes comes closer to approximating that which God has promised. Suffering that produces the ability to accept suffering produces a tested ground from which one may hope.

Hope is constructed slowly, stone by stone. A person who dares to hope must have paid the price in suffering for the ground on which he or she hopes. But the ultimate ground on which the Christian hopes is given by God. No one can guarantee to himself or herself the fulfillment of that for which one hopes. If one could do this, one would not then hope. But Paul assures the Romans that the Christian will not be ashamed for having hoped, because he or she already knows the love of God, which is the ultimate ground on which all hope rests. Christians believe that their hope will not shame them but that it will be validated because God has given them his pledge: he has poured out his love for them into their hearts through the Holy Spirit, whom he has given them. The presence of the Holy Spirit is the guarantee of the fulfillment of our hope—our hope for the glory of God, our hope that we shall be what we were created to be.

Paul then proceeds to describe the occurrence in history that demonstrates to faith the character of the love of God, which is the ultimate source of our hope. He reminds us that it was while we were weak, while we were quite helpless to throw off sin and of ourselves to be restored to peace with God—it was at that time that Christ died for us. An event took place quite outside the realm of our influence, initiated solely by God: Christ died for us. For Paul, the death of Christ was the crucial, all-important factor in making possible reconciliation with God. When he speaks of the love of God, he speaks immediately after of the death of Christ. These two—God's love and Christ's death—were indissolubly linked in his mind. To think of one was always also to think of the other.

That Christ should have died for the *godless* is so extraordinary and incredible a fact that it became for Paul the central point in his understanding of what it was God was doing in Jesus Christ. Paul knew about martyrs, who had given their lives for God, or for a cause, or for people in whom they believed. But self-renunciation involving excruciating pain and death in torture for the benefit of one's *opponents* and *adversaries*—this could be interpreted not as human but only as divine. Christ's act was a divine act, revealing both the love of Christ and the love of God—the same love. His death was both his own offering and the offering of God—the same offering. It is *revelatory* because it was at the same time a human act and a divine act, because what Jesus did and what God did are identical, the human being transparent for the divine.

To look on the love of Christ is to look on the love of God, God's love being revealed to men and women under the conditions of historical existence in the love of a Man who perfectly reflected his own love. And the love revealed by a Man, Jesus, is seen to be *God's* love, because it was expressed in a way contrary to the natural love of natural human beings.

In his lyrical recital of the love of God as manifested in Christ, Paul leaves behind legal and forensic notions of righteousness, the most ultimate thing to be known about God being not that he makes righteous but that he loves.

His righteousness proceeds from his love. In the words of another New Testament author, "God is love."

Paul's discussion of the revealing of God's love in the crucifixion followed from his statement that the Christian can rest secure in hope because it is based on this love. Having, then, portrayed the perfect quality of God's love by recounting its manifestation to us while we were weak, helpless sinners, Paul argues from the greater to the smaller and says that having been acquitted while at our worst we shall surely not be condemned now that we have received God's righteousness. We can rest assured that God will never *withdraw* his love. The love that was revealed at the crucifixion will surely be present at the end, when our ultimate destiny will be revealed.

And this brings us to a further observation. Not only does Paul indicate that our being made righteous is possible only because of Christ's death; he also reminds us that ultimate salvation even for those already reconciled depends on the living Christ. Even the person made righteous cannot go it the rest of the way alone. The reconciliation offered and received in Christ must be received again at every moment, on to the end, when, by Christ, we hope and believe we shall be saved. The Christian, who has been made righteous, who has received peace and the love of God in his or her heart, still hopes and waits for the consummation at the end. Our life, therefore, remains a battle to be fought from day to day, for, as we are admonished by Paul in another letter: "Do you not know that in a race all the runners compete, but only one receives the prize? So run that you may obtain it" (I Cor. 9:24).

For Further Thought . . .

1. Discuss the view that the way in which Paul interprets the Old Testament is not legitimate because he does not interpret the text in accordance with its original meaning.

2. Is it difficult to arrive at the place where one may have hope?

3. Do you agree that hope rests on certain preconditions? Are there other preconditions besides those Paul lists?

4. Paul says that the Christian knows God's love because Christ died for the ungodly (Rom. 5:6–8). What does this statement mean?

CHAPTER 5

Adam and Sin

BEGINNING with Rom. 5:12, Paul offers new evidence for the certainty of salvation, contrasting the work of Adam with the work of Christ, contrasting humanity under sin with humanity under grace. But before we attempt to understand what Paul says about Adam and about sin and death in the world, we should investigate views on these subjects that were held in Judaism in Paul's day and in the period immediately following. Paul quite clearly is assuming and drawing on certain Jewish ideas with regard to Adam, and to sin and death, and before we can understand him we must try to understand something of the soil out of which his thinking developed.

Adam in Genesis

Paul's statement that sin came into the world through one man refers, of course, to sin's entrance through Adam. The story of Adam and of his disobedience of the command of God is found in the second and third chapters of Genesis. We shall not recount this narrative, but it is important for us to notice some aspects of it.

In the first place, Adam is portrayed in Genesis as having been a person who was morally aware before he ate of the tree of knowledge. He is not described in the Garden as being in a state of pre-moral existence. He understands that God has laid a prohibition upon him, and, when he disobeys God, God holds him accountable. Adam is guilty because he "knew better."

In the second place, the story of Adam and Eve in the Garden does not account for the origin of evil. Before Eve transgresses God's command, evil is already present in the serpent, who is wise and subtle. Where the serpent came from, and where he got so many ideas, Genesis does not say.

In the third place, after Adam has eaten the fruit of the tree of the knowledge of good and evil that God has forbidden him to eat, God says, "The man has become like one of us, knowing good and evil." The reference to Adam's having acquired knowledge presumably refers to his new awareness of alternatives, of various possibilities of action that he had not known previously. Thereupon, the fourth chapter of Genesis describes the beginnings of technological and cultural enterprises that followed upon Adam's expulsion from the Garden with his new-found knowledge.

The knowledge gained by eating of the forbidden tree is interpreted by the Genesis author as responsible for the development of civilization—an eventuality that the author regards as unfortunate. It is with the beginning of civilization that the first two cases of hatred and murder occur: Cain kills his brother Abel and Lamech slays a man for wounding him. Slightly later in his story the author tells us that "the wickedness of man was great in the earth."

The point we wish especially to emphasize is that nowhere in this Genesis story is it suggested that Adam and Eve passed on to their descendants an inherent moral weakness because of a change in their nature that took place when they sinned. No change in their nature as it was created by God is indicated. What we are told is that there was disobedience and subsequent gain in knowledge. The sinful acts committed by the descendants of Adam seem to be interpreted by the Genesis author as having their origin in the complexity of the social organism that their knowledge created. The author of the narrative appears to have believed that it was the creation of a complex civilization that led inevitably to mutual hatred in the human race. But the author neither states nor implies that when God expelled Adam and Eve he also altered their nature, making them somehow inherently sinful and all their offspring also prone to sin. On the contrary, Noah, for example, "found favor" in the eyes of the Lord. If the author had believed that all of Adam's descendants were tainted with the sin of Adam, he would scarcely have referred so casually to the favor that Noah found with God.

Finally, let us note that the reason given for God's expulsion of Adam and Eve from the Garden is that God did not want them to eat of the tree of life after they had disobeyed him and gained the knowledge he had forbidden them to have. In other words, God made it necessary for Adam and Eve to die their natural deaths: dust they were and to dust they must return. By nature, from creation, Adam was dust. He was not created immortal. When God drove Adam and Eve from the Garden, he prevented them from being able to perpetuate their lives by eating of the tree of life. Death is not said to have been *introduced* into the world because of sin, but it *must go into effect* because of sin. God acted so as to prevent the race from averting its natural death.

Adam and One's Sin

We have considered briefly a few of the implications of the story of Adam as found in Genesis, implications relevant to our discussion. We must now point out some later developments of this story, some of the emphases with regard to Adam that had developed among Jews of Paul's day.

One development in the story of Adam as it was told through the centuries was that a strong emphasis was put on Adam's disobedience. Now, of course, Adam's disobedience is an important factor in the story as told in Genesis, but in Genesis it is still only one incident in a fairly lengthy narrative that makes other points than that Adam disobeyed.

Another development of the story was that the human race was created immortal but that its immortality was taken from it because of Adam's sin. So, it was believed, death is *inherited*, and because of the close association in the popular mind between death and sin, as well as the relation traced between death and sin in the case of Adam, it was a short step to the assertion that sin is also inherited. One finds many statements in Jewish writings to the effect that there is a bias toward sin, inherited from Adam, to which most people, if not all, are subject.

A third development in Judaism was an ever-increasing idealization of Adam as he was before he disobeyed. There is nothing in particular said about Adam in Genesis that would lead one to believe that he had been a paragon of wisdom and glory, but later stories about him described him in such terms. The increased emphasis on his greatness tended to heighten the catastrophe of his disobedience and prepared the way for the later Christian doctrines of original righteousness and of the calamitous fall.

A fourth element that occasionally emerged in some later forms of the story was that Eve was *seduced* by Satan—seduced in the restricted sense of the word. Thus sin's entrance into the world was related to a sexual act and so sin became a biological factor that was, as such, inheritable. A subsequent development was that sin was a physical taint passed from Satan to Eve and from Eve to all her posterity.

Thus we see that there was a tradition in Judaism relating the sin and death of the race to the sin and death of Adam. This relation was conceived of in different ways by different Jewish authors. Moreover, it is found chiefly in the Jewish apocalyptic writings. The rabbis, who represent what we might call more orthodox Judaism, did not as a rule consider Adam's disobedience to have had any bearing on the sin of humankind. They spoke not of Adam but of the "evil inclination," and it was their view that prevailed in Judaism.

The Jews, under the influence of the rabbis, finally rejected
the apocalyptic writings, which had very little influence on
subsequent Judaism but considerable influence on Christi-
anity.

The "Evil Inclination" and One's Sin

The rabbis, as we have noted, did not account for one's sin
by pointing to Adam. They referred, rather, to what they
called the *yeçer hara,* the "evil inclination." The *yeçer,* that
is, the thought or purpose or disposition of a person, was
believed to have been given by God. It was akin to what
we might call the unconscious. It appears as a dynamic
force, intellectual and emotional, that may be harnessed and
subdued, but that also may destroy. It is called "evil" because if it is not directed by the will as informed by God's
law, it is the power that leads to sin. But as given by God,
the *yeçer hara,* or evil inclination, was thought of as being
essentially good. Referring to Gen. 1:31, "And behold, it
was very good," one of the rabbis commented: "Is, then,
the evil inclination *(yeçer hara)* very good? Certainly, for
without it man would not build a house, or marry, or beget
children, or engage in a trade."

The *yeçer,* then, was understood as the basic energy or
desire that is manifested in the life of all people. It was
believed to be given by God, to be indispensable to human
life, but if not checked it would lead to sin. Therefore, the
rabbis taught that God had also given his law along with the
yeçer—a set of commands and prohibitions that was to serve
as the norm or standard by which one would check and

direct the *yeçer*. One would bring the law to bear on the *yeçer* by the *will*. The *yeçer* provided the basic energy; the *law* described the norm by which the energy was to be directed; and the *will* was to be the agent by which the law would be applied to the *yeçer*.

Even though in popular thinking on the subject the *yeçer* was often construed as evil, this was not the teaching of the rabbis. Furthermore, the rabbis taught that the *yeçer* was implanted individually in each person by God. In other words, the *yeçer* was not believed to be inherited; rather, it was thought to be given by God to each individual separately, either at the time of conception or at the time of birth. So the rabbis did not teach that one inherits a predisposition to sin originating with Adam. On the contrary, they taught that God implants in every person deepseated drives, which one is to control by obeying the law. When one does not succeed in making this basic energy conform to the requirements of the law, one sins. And so far as the race's relation to Adam was concerned, the *yeçer* was not believed to be a predisposition to sin inherited as a result of Adam's sin; it was, rather, the *cause* of *Adam's* sin, as it is the cause of everyone's sin.

On the subject of the cause of death, we find among the rabbis two different views. One view was that in some way the sin of Adam led to death for all people. This idea of universal death was probably related to ancient conceptions of the solidarity of the family, clan, nation, and race, and of the liability of one for all. Thus we find rabbis who taught that Adam's sin involved all his posterity in death. The rabbinic conception of the solidarity of the race was sometimes based on the assumption that all people are derived from one ancestor—Adam. There is thus a unity of all in him. It was in order to emphasize that in Adam all persons are one that strange theories arose concerning the creation of Adam's body. For example, one rabbi taught that God made Adam out of dust gathered from all over the earth. Other speculation claimed that various parts of Adam's body were made from the dust of various geographical regions: his head from Palestinian soil, his trunk from Babylonian soil, et cetera. And in order to include women in the oneness of humankind in Adam, it was taught that Adam was bisexual. So if all people are one in Adam, the fate of Adam must also be the fate of all people.

There was, however, another view represented in rabbinic Judaism—the view that all persons die because all are guilty, that everyone's death is caused by one's own sin. According to this view death came into the world by Adam, who was the first person to die, but every other person has deserved his or her own death. No one has ever fully controlled and directed the "evil inclination" by obeying perfectly the commands of God.

It would probably be true to say that the rabbis of ca. A.D. 100–200 generally taught that Adam's "fall" was not different in kind from the "fall" of every person, that every person relives the fate of Adam. The rabbis certainly did not believe that when Adam "fell" he underwent a change in his nature or constitution that involved his passing on to his posterity a vitiated nature in which the will to good was weakened or totally destroyed. They taught that every person is constituted just like Adam and transgresses just as Adam did. Humanity is Adam, and Adam is humanity.

For Further Thought . . .

1. Discuss the Jewish views of the consequences of Adam's fall, and of the "evil inclination." Do you see any truth in either or both of these views?
2. Do you agree that the human race is a corporate entity and that the destiny of Adam is necessarily the destiny of the race? Illustrate why you do or do not agree.

CHAPTER 6

In Adam or in Christ?

RETURNING now to Paul, we find that he reflects the Jewish teaching—noted in the last chapter—that sin entered into the world through Adam. The fact is quite clear: there was no transgression in the world until the first person transgressed. But when Paul speaks of sin as coming into the world through Adam, he pictures sin as a power, external to Adam, that uses Adam as the means whereby it enters into and then exerts its overwhelming authority over Adam and subsequently over all those who are "in Adam." Sin enters from *outside* into the world of human existence. It "gets in" when it is yielded to, when a person sins. So through "one person" (Adam) the power of sin came to dominate over *all* people.

Secondly, when sin entered into the world, death also entered. Paul again reflects his Jewish background in so closely relating sin and death to each other. When sin came in, death came with it, for to sin is to die. To turn away from God is to reject the Source of life. Paul does not state whether he means that death entered *Adam* when he sinned, or that death entered the *world* when Adam sinned, but he probably means both. Death entered into the world, with sin, as a power over Adam *and* as a power over all other people, who, like Adam, also sin.

We must now point out another element in Paul's discussion. Paul, in a characteristic way, balances his statement about sin as a power external to human beings with another statement. He writes: Sin entered through Adam and death through sin, so that death spread to all people, *because all people sinned.* The italicized words introduce the new idea. Paul has made two statements that balance each other: "death spread to all people" and "all people sinned." The "so that" of the first clause indicates that there is a relation between Adam's sin and death, and all people's sin and death. This relation exists of necessity, because Paul conceives of all people as "in Adam," according to the Jewish conception of the solidarity and unity of humankind in him. We spoke of this unity in the preceding chapter. If Adam sinned and died, then all people who are one in him must also sin and die.

But the second clause states the second truth, which must be placed alongside of the first: "death spread to all people *because all people sinned.*" Each person dies his or her own death because each person commits his or her own particular sins. Paul holds everyone to be personally responsible and personally guilty. Everyone dies because everyone sins.

Paul has made a paradoxical statement about sin and death that represents a view he consistently held. He did not resort to the use of paradox except when he believed that the fullest possible statement of the truth demanded it. In this case, he believes both that all people are individually guilty and therefore individually subject to death, and also that all people, being one in Adam, have sinned and died in Adam.

Closely related to this paradoxical statement is the paradoxical way in which Paul understands sin. For him sin is both a *power* and *transgression.* As a power sin impinges on human beings from the *outside* and exerts its authority over them. As transgression sin is a weakness and perversity and rebelliousness on the *inside* of human beings. It is to sin as a *power* that Paul refers when he speaks of sin's entering the world, and it is to sin as *transgression* that Paul refers when he describes a person's unrighteousness. Sin as power and sin as transgression are, of course, ultimately inseparable. Sin always manifests itself in both ways at the same time and is always experienced in both ways at the same time.

So humankind in Adam is always humankind in sin, both *willingly* (as transgressing) and *of necessity* (as subject to the power of sin). One is not a sinner *exclusively* of necessity. If one were, one would not then be guilty, for one is not guilty because of having yielded to the necessary or inevitable. But one experiences guilt and knows oneself to be guilty. On the other hand, one is not a sinner *exclusively* because one has *willed* to sin. If one were, one could then have been other than a sinner by a change in the will, but it is not one's experience that one can isolate oneself from sin by an act of the will and so avoid guilt. A person cannot side-step sin that incurs guilt by willing to do so. Thus Paul is led by his experience to make a paradoxical statement—that sin strikes as a power external to a person, and that a person transgresses and so is guilty. Because one sins one is subject to the ruling power of death. Without exception, therefore, beginning with Adam, every person has known a law, every person has transgressed the law he has known and has at the same time been subject to the power of sin, and every person has succumbed to the power of death. This has been the pattern from the beginning. The whole of humankind, being one in Adam, has shared inevitably and without exception in Adam's sin and death.

But in Christ, God has offered the race an alternative to sin and death. Humankind may now be one *in Christ* rather than *in Adam.* In fact, a person's oneness in Adam has served only as a prefigurement, as an example beforehand, of the oneness that a person may now have in Christ.

Paul's discussion of Adam and of the race's oneness in Adam, of the race's participation in the sin and death of Adam, has been typically Jewish. Paul did not originate these ideas; nor did he discuss them in his letter to the Romans in order to give the church there a lesson in Judaism. Paul has presented the Jewish view of the oneness of humankind in Adam as an analogy to which he wishes to contrast another unity, in another One, in whom humankind may now find a new ground for its oneness. And the new *possibility* is not like the old *necessity.* As Paul has said before, so he says again, that by the trespass of Adam *all* people died. All people, being one in Adam, sinned and therefore fell under the power of death when Adam sinned. But now the race need not share in the death that was formerly a necessity in Adam. People may participate instead in the gift of life that God offers now as an option in

Christ. The "one man," Adam, brought sin and death for all, but *much more* does God's act of grace and the free gift of the "one Man," Jesus Christ, abound for all.

The judgment following Adam's sin was condemnation for all people, but God's gift in Christ, after many people have trespassed many times, is acquittal. Once again Adam is used as an analogy to Christ. Adam and Christ both acted decisively, but their actions led to opposite consequences: Adam brought condemnation on the race, and Christ brought acquittal for all who will accept it. Death ruled over all because of Adam's sin, but life is now offered to all who will receive it because of Christ's obedience. Christ's whole life may be characterized as a life of obedience to the will of God, but for Paul the major symbol of Christ's obedience was his crucifixion, when he yielded obediently to the demand that he renounce his life.

Paul does not trace the causal relationship between Adam's sin and the condemnation to death that fell on every person; he simply assumes the sickness and the universal death that are the common lot of humankind "in Adam." And we should also observe that whereas one is *born* "in Adam" one is in Christ only by faith. Only those who *accept* acquittal are acquitted. Paul does not assume that when God acted in Christ he acted tyrannically and withdrew from people their freedom. Life is *offered* to all in Christ, but if it is to be had, it must be appropriated.

Yet we must also note another statement that reflects, perhaps, what may have been Paul's belief about one's *ultimate* future. In contrasting Adam's disobedience with Christ's obedience, Paul says that through Adam's disobedience all people were found to be sinners, whereas through

Christ's obedience *all* people will be found to be righteous. Perhaps Paul is looking forward to a day when all humankind will be decreed righteous in Christ, as formerly all humankind was decreed sinful in Adam. Perhaps Paul envisions a time when God will have reconstituted and re-created everyone, receiving everyone in Christ rather than in Adam. Humankind would then be one again: not one in sin but one in righteousness; not one under condemnation but one in acquittal; not one in the death that Adam bequeathed but one in the life that God has freely given through Jesus Christ.

Finally, Paul makes a concluding contrast—the contrast between sin and grace. He refers to the fact, to be developed later, that when the law was given it served only to *increase* trespassing. The law simply multiplied the possibilities of breaking law. Sin therefore increased, but grace abounded still more! One's sin, no matter how pervasive of one's life it has become, has never been an insurmountable obstacle for God, has never estranged one from God to such a degree that God could not get through. There is no darkness so dark that God cannot penetrate it with his light. God's forgiveness has always overbalanced our sin, so that, as sin was decisive in death, the grace of God is all the more decisive over those whom God makes righteous. To them God gives eternal life through Jesus Christ our Lord.

For Further Thought . . .

1. What is the difference between sin interpreted as a power, and sin interpreted as transgression? Do you be-

lieve this to be a valid distinction that corresponds to your own experience?

2. Would you agree with Paul that salvation by means of obedience to the law is impossible?

CHAPTER 7

Dead to Sin and Alive to God

PAUL has been stressing the all-sufficiency of grace—that it is always more powerful than one's sin; that no one is so guilty, so depraved, or so degraded as to be beyond the point where the love of God can prevail. But if this is true, if everyone may, in returning, be welcomed by the Father; if, as sin increases, the grace of God is present in still greater measure, then why not remain in sin? If one will always be forgiven, regardless of one's sin, and if it is pre-eminently one's sin that elicits God's grace, then is there any reason why the Christian should not remain in sin in order "that grace may abound"?

Paul anticipates this question and answers it by saying that the Christian "has died to sin" (v. 2), having been baptized into the death of Christ (vs. 3ff.). In order to understand the significance of these statements we must note briefly two important and characteristic aspects of Paul's thought: his view of the corporateness of humanity, and his belief that corporate humanity is always subject to powers.

The Corporateness of Humanity

"As in Adam all die, so in Christ shall all be made alive" (1 Cor. 15:22). "As by one man's disobedience the many were constituted sinners, so by one man's obedience will the many be constituted righteous" (Rom. 5:19). In these statements, made in two different letters, Paul discloses both of the characteristic elements of his thought just mentioned. In the first place, the race is basically one. Person belongs with person. There is no such thing, ever, as a totally isolated human being. Every person is constituted according to the same principle. Everyone is *in Adam* (if not *in Christ*); therefore everyone participates in the life and destiny of *Adam* (if not of *Christ*).

But since Christ, there are *two* corporate humanities: humanity in Adam, and humanity in Christ. Until Christ came, everyone was in Adam; but since Christ there is a "new creation" in which all humanity is called to live. "For as in one body we have many members, and all the members do not have the same function, so we, the many, are *one body in Christ,* and individually *members one of another*" (Rom. 12:4f.). In Rom. 6 Paul assumes this new corporate humanity which is entered into by being baptized into the death of Christ.

Corporate Humanity as Subject to Powers

But we must also note that for Paul this new corporate humanity in Christ constitutes a new sphere of existence under a new Lord and his power: "Yield yourselves *to God* as people who have been brought from death to life," for you are now "under grace" (vs. 13f.). The old age is characterized by demonic powers; but those in Christ have already been freed from these powers in their acceptance of a new Lord. In Christ one has changed masters. From v. 10 on, Paul repeatedly contrasts two masters, in a parallel way. Primarily the contrast is between slavery to God and slavery to sin (especially in vs. 10–14, 22–23).

Paul thinks of sin as a power, a ruler who claims obedience, just as God does. Formerly *all* people were *under sin* (Rom. 3:9; 6:6). The change that takes place when one is freed from the power of sin is that one changes masters. Then one is enslaved *to God* (6:22). When Paul speaks of "dying to sin" (vs. 2, 10, 11), to which he contrasts "living to God" (vs. 10, 11), both "sin" and "God" are masters to whom one is subject. Hence, to "die with Christ" is to exchange masters: to die to the old master and live to the new one.

Romans 5:12–21 sheds a good deal of light on Rom. 6. In 5:14, 17, 21 sin and death "reign." The same language is used of *grace* in 5:21 and of *sin* in 6:12. The two spheres of influence—one under sin and the other under grace—are connected with Adam and Christ respectively, who are thought of as corporate persons. It is through Adam that sin entered the world and reigns (5:12, 21), and it is through Christ that grace reigns (5:21). The act of Adam (sin) and the act of Christ (obedience unto death) determine the existence of "the many" who constitute each corporate humanity.

This contrast of the two reigns is basic to an understanding of Rom. 6. Christ is the founding figure and corporate person of the new sphere of life, just as Adam was of the old. And Christ's *act* is the foundation of the new humanity (in 5:18–19 the "act of righteousness" and the "obedience" Paul speaks of refer to Christ's death), just as Adam's *act* was of the old humanity.

When Paul says in 6:6 that our "old humanity" (RSV: "our old self ") was crucified with Christ ("old humanity" signifies humanity in Adam), he implies that Christ was *related* to this "old humanity." Further, that the "old humanity" and the "body of sin" (RSV: "sinful body") were destroyed in Christ's crucifixion also implies that Christ was the bearer of this inclusive reality of the old age. Christ was subject to sin (6:10) and death (6:9), as well as to the supernatural "rulers of this age" (1 Cor. 2:8). He was also subject to law and to the "elemental spirits" of the world (Gal. 4:3–5). So while, on the one hand, Christ is for Paul the corporate person of the new humanity, he is also the destroyer of the old humanity. Entrance into the new humanity becomes a possibility for a human being because Christ has dealt the death blow to the *old* one. "Our old humanity was crucified with Christ, so that the body of sin might be destroyed—which makes it possible for us to be no longer enslaved to sin" (6:6).

To be crucified with Christ or to die with Christ is to die to our old humanity as a corporate entity. To "die with Christ" is to die, as Christ did, to sin: as Christ "died to sin"

(6:10), so "we died to sin" (6:2), and "the body of sin" was "destroyed" (6:6). The destruction of the "old humanity" in the cross of Christ meant the death of believers as people of the old humanity. Paul does not speak of the death of individual believers, but of the destruction of the rule of sin under which believers formerly lived.

Of course Paul does not believe that the powers of sin and death no longer exist. The "old humanity" is destroyed in the sense that life in the "new humanity" is now a possibility in Christ. This life is entered into at *baptism*, which for Paul is the crucial saving event in the life of a Christian. The Jew awaits redemption in the future, but the Christian has, in a decisive sense, already been redeemed. Paul's view of the end of this age and the beginning of the age to come, that is, his *eschatology*, may be compared with that of the Jew by the diagrams on the next page. The decisive event for Paul is seen to be baptism.

The Christian's death to sin does not result in a holy nature, or in a state of being that is beyond the attack of sin, but the Christian lives to God "in Christ Jesus." Christians are not dead to sin and alive to God "in themselves." It is in Christ Jesus; it is in the body of Christ—the church; it is by the grace of Christ and by the power of the Spirit whom Christ sends that one may consider oneself to be dead to sin and alive to God. The freedom from sin that is given at baptism cannot be put into one's pocket and possessed; nor can it be shown to a friend. It exists only in relationship to Christ; it is found only where one denies oneself and lets the will of Christ prevail. The Christian is commanded to live *as though* dead to sin, and the Christian is commanded not to submit again to the yoke of slavery to sin. One is,

rather, to offer oneself to God *as* from the dead brought to
life. The word "as" means both "as if one were" and "because one is." In baptism a down payment, a first install-
ment, on redemption is given. At baptism the believer proleptically enters the new age, and proleptically is delivered
from the power of sin and becomes subject to the power of
God. His deliverance is yet to be consummated. Sin is still
an active force, though it has been struck a mortal blow, and
the resurrection for which one hopes is still in the future.
But the Christian has, at baptism, exchanged masters: he or
she is no longer under law but under grace.

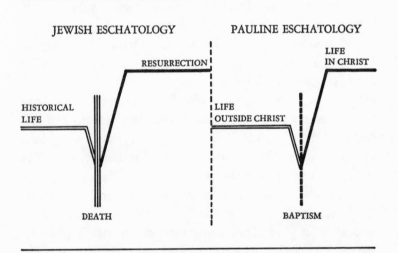

Paul now offers a second explanation of the Christian's
relationship to sin. He has previously said that the Christian
is dead to sin. Now he states that the Christian will not sin
because he or she is not under law but under grace (v. 14).
But this statement needs elaboration, for it *can* be taken to

mean that the Christian does not sin because in Christ one is not ethically committed anywhere, because one no longer stands under any commands and so may do as one pleases. Paul, however, quickly rejects antinomianism (lawlessness) by pointing out that servitude is not an either/or matter, and that subjection to *some* master is inevitable. Deliverance from law—that is, being not under law but under grace—does not mean lawlessness. It does not involve being subject only to whim or passion, or even to one's best-calculated plans for oneself. For Paul every person is subject some-where—outside oneself; no one can be solely a law unto oneself. One may choose the master whom one serves, but the choice of no master at all is not offered. The Christian, then, is not under law, but is still subject. He or she is "under grace." This means that one's life is not oriented to law, to *any* law, but to grace. The believer lives not accord-ing to the commandments of the law but according to God's gift, and the meaning of one's life in Christ is supplied not by one's success in obedience but by one's joy in receiving. The Christian has exchanged masters. He or she is still a slave—a slave no longer to a law that confines and accuses but to God who makes free.

This servitude to God will issue in good fruit. Paul is emphatic in his frequent reiteration of the necessity of faith's bearing fruit. He speaks here three times of obedi-ence or of servitude to "righteousness." This is sometimes felt to be an infelicitous expression. It is said that slavery to righteousness is not very different from the slavery to law, from which Paul has already said the Christian is delivered. But two things must be kept in mind. In the first place, Paul will subsequently give up the slavery metaphor and will substitute a metaphor that more appropriately illustrates the freedom in Christ that he understands the believer to possess. And, secondly, his point here is not to deny the Christian's freedom but to point out to the believer that freedom in Christ becomes possible and is actualized only as one obeys God's one command, which he is later to state as, "You shall love your neighbor as yourself." So the Christian at baptism, and in every succeeding moment of life that calls for a decision, is to die to sin and live to God in Christ Jesus. And the end of those who become "slaves of God" is eternal life. This end, however, is not earned by righteousness. It is, in fact, not earned at all. To "serve righteousness" is to yield fruit; it is not to store up collateral. Sin always pays off in death, but not even the purest goodness leads, in itself, to life. Eternal life, in Christ Jesus our Lord, is a free gift of God.

For Further Thought . . .

1. Discuss Paul's view that every human being belongs to a corporate humanity. Is it true that the destiny of one is the destiny of all?

2. What are the ways in which Christ was related to the corporate humanity in Adam?

3. How does Paul understand freedom to be achieved and manifested?

4. Is the "new life" of a Christian an achievement or a gift?

5. Do you understand your own life as a Christian to be a "new life"?

6. Why is it that good works done under law, rather than under grace, lead only to death?

7. Do you agree that one must always be a "slave"—that is, subject to an external authority?

8. What is the difference between being under law and under grace? What is the difference in terms of one's understanding of one's relation to God? in terms of one's relation to one's neighbor?

CHAPTER 8

The Power of Sin Versus
the Freedom of Human Beings

--- ROM. 7

PAUL has been making the point that the Christian is one
who has changed masters, who is no longer a slave to the
law but has become a slave of Christ. And now, like many
preachers of our own day, Paul offers an illustration, drawn
from contemporary life, of freedom from law; and, as is also
the case in many sermons, the illustration does not quite
make the point. Paul reminds his readers that the law is
binding only on the living. No matter what else may be said
of the dead, at least this much is true: they are no longer
under laws that are binding in historical life. He illustrates
this point by citing the fact that a married woman is bound
by law to her husband as long as he lives, but when he dies
the woman is discharged from this particular law. The illus-

tration obviously is a little off, for it is not the woman but
her husband who dies and thus frees her. But, in any case,
Paul's general argument is clear enough—that at death one
is freed from the law.

Paul then reminds the Roman Christians that they died
to the law, that is, they are not bound to the law any more
than one who has literally died a physical death is bound to
the law. The Christian has died with Christ in baptism. The
believer has died to sin and to the law in order to belong
to another—to Christ. The Christian has changed masters
and in doing so must produce a new and different "fruit."
Our sinful passions had been aroused by the law and the
fruit that we bore led to our death. But now, being set free
from the law, having died to what we had been possessed
by, we are free to bear fruit that leads to life with God.

In saying that the law caused our sin, Paul has come very
close to calling the law itself "sin." And so Paul asks, "Is
the law sin?" He answers strongly that it is not, but he also
adds that he would not have known sin except through the
law. As an example, he refers to the fact that he would not
have known covetousness unless the law had continuously
said to him, "Thou shalt not covet"(v. 7).

Before we continue we should ask who the "I" is in these
verses, and whether it is the "I" *before* faith in Christ, or
after faith. The "I" can, of course, refer to an individual, or
to humanity in general. Undoubtedly it includes Paul, but
undoubtedly also it includes others. The more important
question is whether in these verses Paul is talking about a
person of faith, a believer, and the Christian life; or whether
he is talking about a person *outside* of faith. The arguments
for the former view—that in chap. 7 Paul is describing the

experience of a Christian (which, incidentally, was St. Augustine's interpretation) are as follows:

1. The verbs are in the *present tense.*
2. Chaps. 5–8 all deal with the life of a *Christian,* in connection with sin (chap. 6), law (chap. 7), and death (chap. 8).
3. The words agree with *Christian experience,* as Paul also knew it to be.
4. The difficulty of explaining v. 25*b* (following 25*a)* if the description is of a person outside of faith.
5. The artificiality of much of the chapter if it does not describe Paul's situation *when he is writing* (i.e., in faith). It sounds like pure theatrics on Paul's part if he was not representing his experience at the time he was writing.
6. When Paul describes his former, pre-conversion life as a Jew, there is no trace of this kind of conflict (cf. Gal. 1:13f.; Philip. 3:4ff.).

I confess that for many years these arguments were overwhelming and decisive for me; and in my book, *Romans for the Layman,* as well as elsewhere, I have assumed that chap. 7 refers to the life of a person in faith. But I am now convinced that I was wrong, and have joined the side of the angels. I believe now that the "I" of 7:7–25 describes a person *outside* of faith, but as seen from the point of view of faith. In other words, the section does not fit either (*a*) a person outside of faith as he understands himself (including Paul), or (*b*) the Christian life as Paul understands it. Let us look at some reasons for this judgment.

In the first place, Paul, or the "I," makes statements about himself which a "man in Christ" cannot make: "I am fleshly, sold under sin" (v. 14); or "Nothing good dwells within me, that is, in my flesh" (v. 18). On the contrary, Paul maintains that the person of faith still *does* live *"in* the flesh," though not *"according* to the flesh." And such a person also lives "in the Spirit" and in freedom, and so is *not* "sold under sin." (Recall Paul's words in Rom. 6:2— "You have been *set free* from sin.")

Furthermore, the person of faith no longer cries for redemption from the body of death (7:24); but in faith one knows that "if Christ be in you, although the body be dead because of sin, the Spirit is life because of righteousness" (8:10).

So chap. 7 describes pre-conversion life—but *not* as Paul understood it before his conversion. It is rather Paul's description of the person outside of faith, from the point of view which faith has on unbelief. The words do not describe the self-awareness of a person outside of faith; for as Paul says in 7:15, outside of faith "one does not know what one is doing."

The Meaning of Rom. 7:7–25

Verses 7–8 show how the "I" came to know sin: it was through the law. "Apart from the law sin lies dead." This does not mean that sin does not exist apart from the law; it means that apart from the law sin is ineffectual. When the law appears, sin comes alive. Paul does not deal with the question of where sin (personified) came from. It was simply there before the law.

And these verses do not describe one's *experience* of sin's coming. When one first comprehends sin, it has already been there a long time, and has already done its work. Paul is not depicting empirical experiences, but existential experiences.

"I was alive once apart from the law" (v. 9). Certainly never empirically, though the words are often interpreted that way. It is sometimes argued that Paul is thinking about the innocence of childhood, and then reflecting on his leaving that innocence behind him when he became aware of the law and sin that came later. But totally aside from the dubious assumption of the innocence of children (even of two-year-olds, or *especially* of two-year-olds), for Paul childhood is not a period of life without law—especially as the law is an historical reality: once there, it is always there.

But even if v. 9*a* were interpreted as referring to childhood, what then could v. 9*b* mean: "But the commandment came, sin came alive again, and *I died"?* If v. 9*a* refers to childhood, then v. 9*b* can only be understood in psychological terms, meaning "I freaked out when I became aware of the existence of law." But Paul understands "I was living" and "I died" *theologically:* I possessed life, but sin has destroyed me. This is a description, in faith, of life outside of faith: outside of faith life is under sin; the law comes, and it dies.

The trouble with the law is not that its demands are too great and cannot possibly be obeyed. This is not typical of Jewish faith, and it was not Paul's understanding of the law. For Paul the whole direction of the law—the whole program under law—is wrong. And the reason is that in trying to bring about my salvation by obeying the law, I am seeking to establish my own righteousness—I am coveting. In

obeying the law that says, "Thou shalt not covet," I AM
COVETING. Paul says that in *not* coveting, he was coveting
his righteousness, he was coveting his standing with God.
He had ulterior motives for obeying the law—his enhanced
position before God. Standing under the law, and *obeying*
it, he was at cross purposes with it. So the law makes it clear
that one is in conflict with oneself: one is obeying the law
in order to achieve one's own righteousness. Sin identifies
a person precisely as one who has nothing to show before
God and must turn toward grace.

Paul does not speak of overwhelming guilt under law—
as Luther did. Rather, under law Paul was "blameless"
(Philip. 3:4ff.). It is only by hearing the gospel and the
promise of righteousness by faith that the desperate situation of humanity under law is disclosed. Paul tries to show
that one's real situation in the world under law is hidden—
we do not know what we are doing. We believe we can
serve God by obeying the law. But *after* one believes one
sees that from the beginning the *end* of the law was *faith*
(Rom. 10:4; cf. Gal. 3:24).

Rom. 7:15–20

A common interpretation of this section of chap. 7 is that
Paul is referring to a split between *good intentions* and *evil
doing,* between *will* and *act.* So it is said that a person is split:
one *wishes* to *fulfill* the commandments, but the *doing transgresses* them. For example, I *wish* to stop smoking, but I *do*
not. And Paul is often understood to be making this point
in these verses—but, I think, mistakenly. The basic problem

of one under law is not, for Paul, that one wishes to obey but fails. Paul knows that the situation of one under law is often the opposite—one believes one is *righteous:* not that one's actions do *not* conform to one's will, but that they *do* conform. So one's real situation is hidden.

For light on Paul's understanding of this point, recall Jesus' story of the Pharisee and the tax collector in Luke 18:9–14. The Pharisee's situation is not describable as a conflict between will and performance. He has no conflict in this respect; on the contrary, he believes his will and his performance correspond. He thanks God that he does precisely what he wills to do. But his real situation in the world, under law, is hidden from him—says Jesus. He thinks that in obeying God's commandments he reconciles himself to God; but Jesus says of him that he did *not* go down to his house forgiven.

So also Paul says of himself that as a Jew, under law, he was blameless (Philip. 3:6); but being blameless under law is not identical with being reconciled to God. As a Jew Paul did not know that; but having heard the gospel he *now* knows it. So the answer to the problem of one's estrangement from God is not repentance for transgressions one has committed, but is to renounce altogether one's zeal for the law. Life under law is wrong, not because the law is not kept, but because the whole direction of the way under law is perverse and leads to the establishment of one's own righteousness. In Rom. 10:3 Paul says: "Being *ignorant* that they have righteousness *from God,* they seek to establish *their own.*" And to the Philippians he wrote in a similar vein: ". . . not having a righteousness of *my own,* based on law, but that which is through faith in [or, *of*] Christ, the righteousness *from God* that depends on faith." "By faith" means "by renouncing one's own righteousness." To be made righteous "by faith" is to be made righteous by renouncing all the righteousness which, under law, is "gain" (cf. Philip. 3:7–9).

Hence the division that Paul describes is not between two subjects in the "I"—one fighting against the other; it is not a tension between two forces within a person. The *whole person* is under sin—not just some part. The whole person desires life, and the whole person fails to find it. What one *wills* ("I do not do what I *will,*" v. 15) is not to obey the commandments, but is life. One wants *life.* What one achieves under law, however, is *death*—separation from God.

As a believer, from the point of view of faith, one sees that when one was under law, one willed to achieve righteousness before God, but in fact one achieved the "very thing one hated"—that is, death. Paul does not say that I sometimes fail despite the fact of my good will; nor does he say that I fail completely; nor does he say that there is a remnant of selfishness in every good deed. The problem in human life is more basic than this: the problem is that I am constantly seeking the good (that is, life), and that I am equally constantly failing, and necessarily so because my very striving for righteousness under law leads to death. "I do not do the good I wish, but I do the evil that I do not wish" (v. 19). The object of "willing" is "life"; but the result of "doing" is "death." This is one's experience—not while one is under law, but later, from the point of view of faith in Christ.

The chapter ends in a lament: "Wretched I, a human

being! Who will rescue me from this body of death?" These
words do not come from the mouth of Paul the Christian
who has been tempted and has yielded to the power of sin.
Paul is not describing a psychological reaction to a moral
setback. The significance of this lament may be clarified if
we look for a minute at the lament of the soul in gnosticism.
The gnostic believed that in this world a human being is in
a deadened state of unknowingness, understanding neither
himself nor the world. But one is aroused by a cry from
heaven, similar to the cry in Ephesians: "Awake, O sleeper,
and arise from the dead, and Christ shall give you light"
(Eph. 5:14). On hearing such a cry the gnostic perceives
with horror that he or she has been thrown into an alien
world, and cries out in a lament. The lament indicates that
one has become aware for the first time of who one is, and
where one is; and being aware, the gnostic may then begin
his ascent back into the world of light. In lamenting one
glances *backward* and laments what *has been,* not what now
is.

It is perhaps in some such sense as this that we should
understand Paul's lament in v. 24. Paul the Christian who
in Christ, for the first time, understands his real situation in
the world, glances backward and places this lament in the
mouth of Paul the Jew. In this way he establishes the conti-
nuity that exists between the unbeliever and the believer.
The believer is not called to light (like the gnostic), but is
called to faith, and knows that he or she has been delivered
from the "wretchedness" of the past in Jesus Christ. The
lament comes after hearing the gospel, and is followed
immediately by a thanksgiving: "Thanks be to God through
Jesus Christ our Lord!"

In concluding our discussion of this chapter, we may say that for Paul sin is basically one's wanting to run one's life, to manipulate it, to dispose of it oneself; it is making claims for oneself, seeking righteousness by works, based on law. Instead of the "I," sin becomes the subject. One can be one's self, however, only when one surrenders oneself to God in Christ, when one exists only from God in Christ, when one accepts righteousness that is not one's own, by faith.

For Further Thought . . .

1. Do you believe that Paul is describing Christian life, or life outside of Christ in Rom. 7?
2. Why does Paul say that it is wrong to seek to establish my righteousness before God? Aren't we taught from early childhood that who we are depends on what we make of our lives?
3. Is it necessary to understand oneself as a sinner before one is able to receive the salvation offered in Christ? What is Paul's view? What is your view?

CHAPTER 9

Adopted in Love

————————————————————————————————————— ROM. 8

"THEREFORE, now, there is no condemnation for those who are in Christ Jesus." There is no condemnation "now" because "in Christ Jesus" one has "died to sin" (6:2) and been "freed from sin" (6:7). One is "not under law but is under grace" (6:15); one has changed masters and belongs to the new humanity in Christ, rather than in Adam. In Christ one is accepted by God, which makes it possible also for one to accept oneself.

It is not the case that God's acceptance depends upon the self's prior achievement of a harmony within itself that merits his acceptance; it is rather the case that God in Christ accepts a divided, estranged, and hostile self and offers it the possibility of harmony and wholeness. A guilty child cannot make herself not guilty before she returns to her mother's love, but a mother may receive back a guilty child in love and so restore wholeness and peace where there had been division, estrangement, and guilt. In a like way, Paul tells us that God in love has received us back with no punishment entailed, thus offering us a new beginning in a new community in which we are accepted as we are and in which, therefore, we may accept ourselves. Self-acceptance cannot precede God's acceptance, but it will follow, if we seek to be accepted and believe that we have been.

But does God offer estranged human beings any possibility of knowing, in history, that he has accepted them, and any possibility, therefore, of their being able to accept themselves and so function as whole rather than as divided selves? Paul's answer to this question is that God gives the *Spirit* to those who are in Christ Jesus, and to have received the Spirit, or to live in Christ Jesus, is to be set free from the power of sin and death. Formerly sin and death were inevitable. Sin, in using the law, had brought death to all. But in Christ one is raised out of the old inevitability of sin and death into a new possibility of righteousness and life.

God sent his Son into the world in the form of flesh, to deal with sin. It may be that Paul thinks of Christ as having been a sin offering made by God, but in any case Paul believed that through Christ in the flesh God had condemned sin. The power of sin was broken when it attempted to bring Christ to defeat. In Christ, God triumphed over sin, raising his Son from the dead. And those who are in Christ, who have died and been raised with him, have been delivered over, out of the bonds of sin, into the hands of him who has condemned sin and who re-creates life. These are the believers who do not walk "according to the flesh" but who walk "according to the Spirit."

Paul refers to *flesh* and *Spirit* as opposites. They represent

two contrasting ways of "walking," two opposite directions
in which one may live. "Flesh" and "Spirit" describe, for
Paul, contrasting orientations open to human beings, and
one's destiny depends on the orientation one chooses for
oneself. If one's intentions, one's motives, one's endeavors,
one's direction are according to the flesh, the end is death.
But if one's intentions, motives, endeavors, and direction
are according to the Spirit, the end is life and peace.

To live according to the flesh is to be oriented toward the
world and away from God, is to seek one's own righteousness. It is to seek to find one's life among the created things
of the world, rather than in the Creator. The end of such
seeking must be death, because the world—the things of
the world—cannot offer life. Not even the law, being also
a created thing, can give life, for sin uses it to destroy. One
who lives according to the flesh, who is oriented to the
flesh, cannot please God and cannot find life.

But to strive according to the Spirit, to be oriented toward the Spirit, is to be oriented away from the world and
toward God. It is to look away from created things, in the
direction of the Creator, for life. Those who are "in the
Spirit" are those who find life not by obeying the law but
by accepting God's acquittal. They have learned that they
cannot earn life or create it for themselves but that God, in
Christ, offers life as a free gift.

To walk by the Spirit is also to have grounds for the
assurance that the life now offered in Christ will be fulfilled
at the end, for the Spirit is the guarantee of the consummation. The giving of the Spirit was contingent on the resurrection, and the presence of the Spirit in the church attests
the reality of the resurrection. Hence the reception of the

Spirit by the believer is the ground of the believer's hope that he or she will participate in the resurrection of Christ. And so the Spirit gives life to the believer in the present and is also the source of the believer's hope for the future fulfillment of the life already received proleptically.

Through the Spirit one is related to God in an altogether new way. Paul characterizes this new relationship as one of *sonship*. Those who are led by the Spirit of God, those who are in Christ, those who have received righteousness as a gift and have given up striving to earn their own salvation are children of God. A Christian is related to God as a child. *This* relationship is not a *natural* relationship that a human being has with God simply by virtue of being born. It is not a birthright but a relationship that God *gives,* in Christ, to anyone who will receive it. Children of God are children by *adoption:* they have been bought with a price.

It is, then, God's adopted children who have received the Spirit. And it is by the Spirit that one knows oneself to be an adopted child, for it is by the Spirit that one relates oneself to God as a child to a parent. To know God as Father is to have received the Spirit, and to have received the Spirit is to have been adopted as a child. Sonship equals relationship to God via the Spirit.

To be adopted as a "child" by a "Father" is to be incorporated into a new relationship in which the ultimate meaning of life is revealed, in which life is transformed and re-created. If a lost and lonely child is adopted by a family, then, because of belonging in a family, all is not lost if he or she fails in an undertaking. One may accept the failure as a failure and transcend it, because of a more significant relationship one has to parents who love one. The child is enabled to accept himself or herself *with* the failure, because he or she, *with* the failure, has been accepted by others in love. And if a child who has been adopted *succeeds* in some enterprise, the joy will not be emptied by loneliness but will be increased in the home when it is shared in love.

So, also, with the Christian. The Christian as an adopted child is incorporated into a new community, the church, in which God is known as Father. In this community, if the children are indeed children, sorrows are transcended and joys are heightened—life is re-created. The whole community has been adopted by God, called into being by his Spirit, whom all children share alike. All the members of the community were lonely and forsaken and lost until God adopted them into the household of faith. Now they need no longer seek acceptance, for they are already accepted, else they would not be children. Now they need no longer prove themselves, for they are loved *before* they succeed— or fail. The church is the community of the redeemed. This does not mean that its members are morally perfect; it means that they have been given life and have found themselves because they have been found by God.

And now Paul says one further thing about believers. As children who have been adopted, they are also *heirs*—heirs in possession and heirs apparent. Those who suffer with Christ are those who will also be glorified with Christ. The adopted children are to share in the glory of the eternal Son. The Holy Spirit is God's *pledge* that the inheritance will be received. It is the down payment, a foretaste of what is to come.

We have mentioned that those who *suffer* with Christ are

heirs with Christ. It is clear that, to Paul, being a child in possession of the Spirit does not exclude suffering. On the contrary, sonship involves suffering with Christ—suffering not as an end in itself but as a prelude to glory. Sharing the glory is contingent on sharing the suffering. The raised One was first crucified. But the suffering that the Christian must bear in the name of Christ is nothing in comparison with the glory that is yet to be revealed. The Christian's life in the present is ambiguous; but the fulfillment for which he or she hopes is not ambiguous. In the present there is *both* suffering *and* a foretaste of the good things to be revealed, but in the future the Christian is promised glory with Christ. The deposit on the future has been made, the Spirit has been given, the love of God has been revealed, and we with endurance await the consummation.

While we wait we are supported by the Spirit, who intercedes with God on our behalf with inarticulate sounds, and God knows that the intention of the Spirit is to intercede with him according to his will. Furthermore, we are persuaded that God himself is working with those who love him toward the good end that he has promised all those whom he calls. And, finally, Christ Jesus, who died and was raised and is at God's right hand, is also interceding for us. The whole creative and merciful power of God is on our side! We are convinced that nothing will ever be able to separate us from God's love. The life that has been given will be given again in full measure. God who loved us when we were unlovable, and gave his Son for us, and raised him from the dead, will raise us up also and make us to share with Christ in glory. And all this is from God, through Jesus

Christ—righteousness and peace, and hope for the day when the love of God shall have reconciled the whole creation to itself and to its Creator.

For Further Thought . . .

1. How does the Christian know that God works with him or her toward good?
2. What price has been paid so that people may be adopted as children of God? *From* what are they adopted, and *to* what are they adopted?
3. Think of an example of the difference between walking "according to the flesh" and walking "according to the Spirit."
4. Explain why the metaphor of "adoption" is a good one for the Christian's understanding of his or her new life.

CHAPTER 10

Are Jews Also to be Saved?

ROM. 9 TO 11

PAUL has described the plight of all human beings, both Jews and Gentiles, and he has elaborated the gospel that he preaches—the good news that God has acted in Jesus Christ to redeem those who cannot redeem themselves. By faith one may now be reconciled to God; by faith one may have righteousness and peace. God has revealed his love for us —a saving love from which, if we will receive it, nothing in the whole creation will be able to separate us.

But Paul is deeply grieved by the fact that his own people according to the flesh—the Israelites—have not been willing to appropriate the gift that God has offered in Christ. The Jews prefer their own way—the way of following the law—a way that, as Paul has shown, leads only to destruction. Paul is grieved by the stubbornness of his kinsfolk, because he knows that they are cutting themselves off from salvation. No one who refuses the *gift* of salvation in Christ can be saved, but the Jews still insist that, to put the matter as Paul sees it, they, of themselves, can *earn* their own salvation by their obedience to the law.

And so Paul has constant pain in his heart for his "kinsmen according to the flesh," on behalf of whom he would gladly cut himself off from salvation in Christ. But Paul is not only grieved; he is also perplexed by a theological problem raised by his people's self-exclusion from the church. The problem may be put in the following way: If the Israelites are the heirs of God's promises, as according to Scripture they are, then how does one explain the fact that they have not received the fulfillment of God's promise in Jesus Christ? Did God fail to forsee that in the end Israel would *not* participate in the salvation he had promised? Or, did he make Israel promises he knew would never be fulfilled? This is the theological problem to which Paul now turns. What is to happen to the Jews, the people whom God chose but who are now outside of the community of the redeemed?

Paul begins his discussion of this problem by noting, as he has before, that not all descendants of Abraham are necessarily Israelites. The real descendants of Abraham are children of the promise and not children of the flesh. Paul shows that this view of who belongs to Abraham's posterity and who does not is scriptural. He reminds his readers that by Sarah, Abraham had a son, Isaac; then Isaac had two sons, Jacob and Esau, who were twins, both of whom were, of course, descendants of Abraham. The twins had the same mother and father, and were both grandchildren of Abraham; yet one was chosen and the other was not. Esau was to serve Jacob. This distinction between Jacob and his twin brother was made before they were born. Jacob was loved and Esau was hated, but not because of anything either had done. The choice of Jacob was made before either of them had come into the world. Jacob was a true Israelite; Esau was not. Jacob was heir of the promises made to Abraham; Esau was not. The rejection of Esau shows, says Paul, that blood descent from Abraham does not guarantee election. Furthermore, as the choice of one twin over the other was made before their birth, it is also clear that God's election is not dependent upon or related to one's performance—one's virtue or one's sin—but is an absolutely free act. Lineage cannot guarantee election; nor does election presuppose righteousness; but God's election is, rather, a free act of mercy. If either lineal descent or ethical performance could guarantee election, then God's choice would not be *free* and would not be an act of *mercy*. Hence, at the beginning of his discussion, Paul has us understand that however God's relation to the Jews be interpreted, his freedom and his mercy must not be compromised in the slightest degree.

Paul has shown that no one is ever in a position to *claim* salvation, no matter what his or her lineage—not even the Jew, and perhaps we might add not even the person enrolled as a church member. Salvation is given in mercy, and not across the counter. Can one then retort that God's mercy is accorded arbitrarily and that God is therefore unjust? Paul's immediate answer to this question is that mercy is never unjust, that a sheer gift in love and compassion transcends the category of justice. Justice involves weighing what is due. Mercy transcends calculation; it is not based on merit. Whether mercy is bestowed, or is not bestowed, is not, then, a matter of justice at all.

But Paul goes on to show that there is purpose behind
God's *not* showing mercy, and that this purpose also is
governed by mercy. He quotes scripture again, citing God's
purpose in raising up Pharaoh, to whom he did not show
mercy. But God's purpose was nevertheless motivated by
mercy, for Pharaoh provided the occasion for God to deliver his people from bondage, as well as the occasion for
the proclamation of this deliverance throughout the world.
The parallel intended between Pharaoh and the Jews is
clear: the Jews' rejection of the gospel has provided the
occasion for the deliverance of the Gentiles and for the
proclamation of the gospel in all the earth. The purpose
lying behind God's action in history is not always immediately understandable, but Scripture reveals it to be always
controlled by his mercy.

The situation in the present is, then, that the Gentiles,
who did not strive to earn their own righteousness by per-
fecting their moral life under the law, have been *given*
righteousness, have been acquitted by God and accepted by
God as righteous. The Gentiles have attained righteousness
in the only possible way in which it can be obtained,
namely, by faith, that is, by accepting it as a gift from God
through Jesus Christ. But the Jews, who pursued righteousness by obeying the law, have not attained it. They have
stumbled over Christ rather than finding life through him.

Paul here gives his second explanation of why the Jews
stand outside the salvation that is offered in Christ. His first
answer was that God is absolutely free in the bestowal of his
mercy. This freedom with which God shows mercy does not
in any way compromise or restrict his mercy. He is not less

merciful because he is free in his granting of mercy; on the contrary, *all* his acts are done in mercy. But Paul's second explanation of the predicament of the Jews is that they have themselves chosen to reject God's mercy. There is a polar unity, never clearly perceived by the human mind, between God's action and human action, between God's freedom and human freedom. Paul does not try to explain by a neat, logical formula how it can be that both God and human beings are free, or, to put it another way, how God's omnipotence and predestination are related to humankind's freedom and responsibility. There is no logical, rational explanation of this relationship. A logical resolution of it would require compromising the freedom of God, or of human beings, or of both God and humankind. Such a resolution, dictated by logic, would be compelling if one's experience could confirm it. But one experiences both a determining power outside oneself and a personal freedom and responsibility, which will not permit one's acceptance of the only answer logic can offer. And so Paul combines two answers to the question of why the chosen people are not included among those who have been made righteous in Christ: *(a)* God chooses whom he wills, and *(b)* the Jews have rejected God's offer. Both answers are intended to apply not in a sequence but *at the same time.* To put the situation in another way: God provided the stone on which Israel stumbled, and Israel is responsible for stumbling over the stone.

Paul now elaborates the second aspect of his answer to the theological question with which he began, namely, the Jews' personal responsibility for their existence outside the community of faith. The Jews have not been willing to receive righteousness as a gift; they have been willing only to establish their own righteousness. This means, from Paul's point of view, that they have not been willing to be *in debt* to God for their salvation. They have refused to acknowledge the fact that to accept salvation is *necessarily* to be in debt, but they are persisting in their attempt to be able to pay their own way through the "pearly gates."

To be sure, until Christ came righteousness was only possible in terms of obedience to the law, but Christ has put an end to this. He has come; he has been raised from the dead; and *faith,* in contrast to *works,* is now a possibility for everyone—including the Jew. It is through *faith* that one is made righteous, but the Jews still will not accept this; they will not be obedient to the gospel.

Paul now shows, in concluding his discussion of the Jews' responsibility, that his people have long been disobedient, and that their rejection of the salvation that the Gentiles would accept was already forseen by Moses. Israel's own Scripture shows that Israel was at the same time an elect people and a disobedient people. It was always both lost and found, both chosen and rejected. The beloved children of God were a disobedient and contrary people. This is Israel's history.

Hence Paul puts the question, "Has God rejected his people?" He returns again to the first aspect of his answer to the question of the plight of the Jews, to a consideration of the freedom and mercy of God. We have already seen that the election of Israel has always had an ambiguous character. Israel has always been both chosen and disobedient. Is its present disobedience, therefore, so different in degree from its past disobedience that it can no longer participate in God's election? Is it possible that the Jews' freedom can ultimately prevail over God's freedom? Is God's freedom to choose conditional? Or, does God reject those whom he formerly chose and is his election temporary or contingent? These are the questions with which Paul now wrestles.

Turning, then, to the question of whether God has rejected his people, Paul answers, in the first place, that quite obviously he has not—at least not all of them. For Paul himself is a Jew, and he has been reconciled in Christ. And there are other Jews who also believe in Christ—Jewish Christians. There is, then, a *remnant* of Israel that has not been rejected and that has been incorporated in the "New Israel." God has kept these few Jews for himself as in the days of Elijah he had kept for himself the seven thousand men who would not bow the knee to Baal.

But what about the *majority* of the Jews—Israel as a whole —has God ultimately rejected them? Paul answers that God most assuredly has not but that his dealing with the Jews, like all his acts, must be understood in terms of his mercy. The Jews stumbled: their eyes do not see and their ears do not hear. But, because they have rejected the gospel, it has been preached to the Gentiles. Thus through the trespass of the Jews salvation has been made possible for the Gentiles. The Jews' failure to believe has meant great riches for the non-Jews. Paul, however, forsees the day when the Jews, having become jealous of the election of the Gentiles, will return and believe. At the end of the age, before the dead are raised, the Jews whom God has rejected will be accepted.

Paul takes the opportunity to remind the Gentiles that they had better not boast of their new status of acceptance.

They are reconciled now only by faith and are not so secure that God in his freedom cannot reject them! If God did not spare the Jews, it is an eventuality to be reckoned with that he will not spare the Gentiles either! A person, in the presence of God, can never have what the world calls security; he or she can never know what the world calls certainty. A person before God is always a person in hope, a person at prayer, a person with empty hands outstretched to receive for nothing a gift from the Giver of life. One's hope, one's expectation, one's certainty can only be in One other than oneself. They can never, therefore, be self-initiated, self-preserved, or self-vindicated. Hence the Gentiles, the elect of God who have been made righteous by faith, dare not boast!

The Jews have become enemies of God for the sake of the Gentiles. But God originally called the Jews, and his call is irrevocable. When God calls, he calls in freedom. His call is not summoned by a righteous people and is not withdrawn from an unrighteous people. As with God's call, so with his mercy: one can neither bid it come, nor bid it go. Paul has seen a mystery revealed: the Jews have been rejected for the sake of the Gentiles and for the sake of their own reacceptance on the basis of faith. They will learn the lesson that all must learn if they are to be saved, namely, that to seek to *earn* God's mercy is to resist it.

But who can fully comprehend these things? Who has known the mind of the Lord? Before whose eyes has God revealed the beginning and the end, the totality of all things that are or ever shall be? Israel has been chosen by God and has responded so as to be received as his own people; it has also been rejected by God and has denied him at the moment of his final revealing. The Gentiles have been rejected by God and have failed to honor him as God; they have also been called out by God and have responded to him in faith. Who can understand the merciful acts of God? What will the end of all things be? Paul can only exclaim that God's judgments are unsearchable and that his ways are inscrutable! But we can know this: that God is free—always, and that he is merciful—always. We can know that whatever happens has its beginning and end in him. More than this we cannot know now. We can only give God the glory, both now and forever.

For Further Thought . . .

1. What is the relation between the idea of God's election "not because of works but because of his call" (Rom. 9:11), and the idea of being made righteous by faith?
2. Referring to particular verses of Romans 9 to 11, answer the following questions:
   a. Why have the Jews rejected the gospel?
   b. What is God's intention for the future destiny of the Jewish people?
   c. Does God ever go back on his promises?
   d. Is the destiny of Israel the same as the destiny of the Gentiles who are in Christ?
3. Discuss the view that God's election cannot be unjust because it is an act of compassion.

CHAPTER 11

Only One Commandment

PAUL moves now to a discussion of the conduct of Christian life and to a few ethical questions. We have already observed that Paul is not antinomian, that he does not advocate chaos in the ethical life of Christians. On the contrary, he believes that Christians, as those who have died with Christ, have died to their old selves and have accepted a new Lord. To this new Lord, Jesus Christ, Christians owe obedience. In fact, in Paul's writings *faith* includes *obedience*. The person of faith, the believer, is a slave of Jesus Christ.

But Christians are not only slaves, who owe obedience; they are also adopted sons, incorporated into a new community of love. They have been bought with a price; they have been found and have been brought to the home in which they may also find themselves. The Christian's response to the love that has redeemed him or her is *gratitude*. The believer has not earned adoption, but should be grateful for

88

it. One cannot buy one's way into the community of love by offering so much in the way of good performance; nor can one claim to have any *rights* there; but one can be grateful for having been taken in, and can love in response to the love that has loved one. The Christian is obedient, not as one whipped into submission, but as one who, being loved, acts in gratitude according to the will of him who loves one. As one who has died with Christ and been raised with him, the believer is one who has turned his life over to Christ. One strives to bring all one's thought and action into conformity with the will of God as it has been made known in Christ.

Paul's theology will not permit him to draw up a "Christian" ethical code. For him, the phrase "Christian ethical code" would be self-contradictory. The Christian is *freed* from all codes of ethics, from all systems—obeying not a code but a Person, not the letter but the Spirit. Yet one still *obeys*. The Christian is one who seeks to apprehend and to bring his actions into conformity with the mind of Christ. Paul laid down a basic principle, together with some derived principles, which Christians were to apply in arriving at concrete ethical decisions. At the end of his letter to the Romans, Paul states the basic principle—love of neighbor—as well as some derived principles. He also deals with a few particular issues that had arisen in the church at Rome. We shall not note everything Paul says with regard to these matters, but in this and the following chapters we shall consider briefly some of his major points.

We note, in the first place, that the Christians are to offer their whole life to God in sacrifice; that their life is a sacrificed life, life dedicated and handed over to another—to

God, who is merciful. As this age is fast drawing to a close, the believers are not to make their life conform to it but to the will of God, who has already initiated the new age that in the near future will be consummated.

Paul, in the second place, draws the attention of the Christians in Rome to their own peculiar existence as a church. The church is a kind of beachhead on the age to come. A foretaste of this coming age has been given by the Spirit, whom the Christians have received, and the Christians as a community are to understand their life together as a manifestation in advance, imperfect but ever maturing, of the life to come. Paul bids the Roman Christians to take their calling as Christians seriously. He tells them that they are to function, to live together, as one body or organism, harmoniously, each performing his or her own particular work with excellence. None should boast of their own accomplishments, but everything should be done in gratitude and with the consciousness that whatever one does has been made possible only by a gift one has received. The gifts God bestows upon believers are given for the benefit of the whole Christian community and not for the increase of the individuals' prestige.

For Paul the church is the body of Christ. It is to function as a unit made up of many separate parts, each of which is to serve the whole. The church is Christ at work in the world, calling men and women to redemption. Each of its parts is to live in harmony with all other parts, no one part believing itself more important than any other, but each knowing that it is able to function only because it is related to the whole.

What does Paul say about the relation of Christians to

their enemies outside the church? Christians are to bless and not curse them, that is to say, they are to hope for and act on behalf of the good of their enemies. Christians are not to return evil for evil, but are to have regard for the honorable thing before all people. In fact, they are not to avenge themselves at all.

With regard to disputes between one Christian and another, Paul wrote to the Corinthians that they should be settled within the church, by a Christian. Believers should not take difficulties that have arisen among themselves to be settled in pagan law courts. Here, in his letter to the Roman church, Paul advises Christians not to take hostile, retaliatory action against pagans. He is not advocating the perpetuation of injustice, but he believes that the state, as an instrument of the wrath of God, will adequately punish pagans who are unjust. The Christian will not be reluctant to see evildoers punished, but will leave it to the civil authorities to do the punishing. The *Christian's* action, however, will be directed toward the *good* of his or her enemy. If good is returned for evil, perhaps the enemy will be won over. In any case, a victory will have been won by the one who has done the good, and the fate of the enemy remains in the hands of God.

Christians, then, as those who are obedient to Christ, are to love their enemies. They know only one Master, and are to bring every thought and action into subjection to him: they are subject only to the Lord. Paul now, in a parenthetical way, deals with the question of the believer's proper relation to civil authorities. If Christians obey only Christ, then how are they to relate themselves to the civil authority under which they live? Paul's answer to this question is that one is obliged to be subject to the authority of the state. Why should this be? Because all civil authority is derived from God. There is only one authority—the authority of God—and all other authorities exist only if God has established them. Hence the authority of the state has been instituted by God. This being the case, all people, including Christians, must be subject to it. One who resists civil authority is an evildoer, and the state, as a servant of God, will avenge the wrong because it is an instrument of the wrath of God. In the world as God has created it, one must be subject to authority, and if one resists, one will be not only externally punished by the state but also internally punished by the conscience.

Does Paul reveal a total ignorance of the workings of the state when he affirms that earthly rulers need cause no fear to those who do good, but only to those who do evil? Is he utterly naïve with regard to the immoral, tyrannical ways in which the state often exercises its power? Hardly so! He knows as well as anyone that it was by command of the Roman state that Jesus was crucified. He also knows, however, that Jesus did not resist Roman power. He further knows that even on that dark Friday the authority wielded by Rome was ultimately the authority of God, for it was *God* who there on Calvary offered up his Son "for us men and for our salvation." Paul was neither ignorant nor naïve with regard to the authority of the Roman state. For theological reasons he could not radically divorce earthly authorities from the authority of God.

It would be a mistake to assume that Paul's advice to the Roman Christians was given for pragmatic reasons—because, for example, he believed that to submit to the state would be personally beneficial and therefore the prudent thing to do. This had not been Jesus' experience; nor was it Paul's. It was *in spite of* the consequences and not *because of* them that Paul exhorted subjection to the authorities.

One other factor should be borne in mind in attempting to understand Paul's position. Paul believed that the day of God's reign was already dawning. The present historical age that Paul characterizes as "the night" was about over. This being the case, he believed that all earthly authorities were approaching the end of their existence. They were temporary structures through which God maintained order and exerted his wrath, but their period of service was expiring. Paul, though he exhorted submission to these author-ites, also believed that in the very near future they would be things of the past.

And so the believers are to subject themselves to civil authority. They are to pay their taxes, and anything else they may owe, for they are not to be in debt to anyone. Christians are to owe no one anything; they are only to love one another. All the commands are summed up in this one statement: "You shall love your neighbor as yourself."

Paul has elaborated at some length on the Christians' deliverance from the law, and on the fact that, in dying with Christ and being raised with him, they are acquitted by God and made free to obey in faith. Their acquittal is dependent not upon ethical performance but upon their willingness to accept God's free offer of life. If one accepts this offer, then one gives up the possibility of making any claims for oneself and accepts both one's own unworthiness and the worth that one is accorded by the love of God. The Christians' response to the reconciliation into which God has brought them is one of gratitude. With a grateful heart, and with a joy and peace they had not known before, the believers accept Jesus as their Lord. What, then, is their ethical responsibility? It is not to obey the law from which they have been freed—a law that had enslaved them and under which they had been condemned. The Christians are subject, rather, to a new law—new because it is for them now the only law, the law of their being that does not enslave their life but enables it to be fulfilled—the law of love. This law is not a law in the old sense of the word, for it neither restricts freedom nor circumscribes the full expression of life. Nor does the law of love divide people into hostile groups made up of those who obey it and those who do not, the self-righteous and the sinners. On the contrary, to obey the law of love is to be united with one's neighbor and not estranged from him or her. And to obey this law is to be free.

The Greek word Paul uses here for love is *agapē*. It is a word for which we have no exact equivalent in English and with which we should become familiar. The English language, which in many ways is so rich, is at this point rather poor. We use the word "love" to express our desire for union with anything or anyone. We love a certain food; we love Beethoven's music; we love our friends; we love our children; we love God; and God loves us. It is most unfortunate that we must use the same word to describe all these relationships. But in the Greek language the situation was somewhat different. There was a word *(epithumia)* that expressed one's desire for material things. There was a different word *(erōs)* that was used to characterize desire for union with the beautiful and the true. Then there was a third word *(philia)* that described the desire of the self for another self, the word used to describe the relationship in love between persons. Paul's word was still another word. It was a word that received its meaning in the early church and was hardly known before the church used it. This word, *agapē*, was used to describe God's relation to humankind as it was revealed in Jesus Christ. *Agapē* is love that enters into historical life from another dimension—from God. It is not natural love, not love that one has by nature, but the love with which *God* loves in Jesus Christ. God, who *is agapē*, manifests himself as *agapē*.

For a person to love in the sense of *agapē* is for him or her to love in response to God's love. It is, then, with the love wherewith God loves us that we are commanded to love our neighbor. We are not to love him because we are attracted to him, or because he has worth in our eyes, but only because God loves him. Our neighbor, that is, any person with whom we may come into contact, is one for whom Christ died, and as such a one we too ought to love him if we count ourselves among those for whom He died.

What can it mean to love people if one is neither physically attracted to them, nor intellectually impressed by them, nor at home in their presence? *Agapē* affirms as a person everyone who is met, and sees that person as God sees him or her. Neither admiration, nor physical attraction, nor sympathy is required on our part. *Agapē* involves self-sacrifice, not for the sake of the neighbor as he is, but for the sake of his ultimate destiny. And so *agapē* always contains an element of forgiveness. It forgives the neighbors as they are, and sees them as they might be and as, by the grace of God, they will be.

Agapē is essentially, as we have said, God's love for us. We cannot initiate it, but we can respond to it. And the believer's response to the love of God is his love for the neighbor, for whomever he meets. The command, "Love your neighbor," means, "Let the love of Christ control you," or, "Love with the love of God that has been poured into your hearts." *Agapē* takes its definition from Christ, is known through Christ, and draws one to Christ.

Paul also says of *agapē* that it is the fulfillment of the law. If one loves in the sense of *agapē,* one does what the law requires—God's law and the law of one's own being. In saying this, however, Paul is not instituting a new legalism. He does not say that if one loves, one will be made righteous; he says that if one has been made righteous (acquitted), one ought to love. Love does not *lead to* reconciliation with God; it *follows from* reconciliation. For one cannot initiate *agapē;* one can only receive it as a gift and respond to it. Hence it is evident that *agapē,* which is purely *responsive* love on one's part, cannot *lead to* acquittal. It *presupposes* acquittal. It is possible only "by faith," or "by grace," or "by the Spirit." One is not justified *by loving* but only *by faith.* Love is the way in which faith is exercised, the way in which faith works itself out in relation to the neighbor. The believer's relation to Christ *in faith* issues in his relation to his neighbor *in agapē.* To act in *agapē* is to act on the gift of salvation that one has received, is to love because one has been loved.

For Further Thought . . .

1. Discuss the view that the command to love one's neighbor assumes or includes the command to love God.
2. What does Paul mean when he says that if you do good to your enemy "you will heap burning coals upon his head" (Rom. 12:20)? Do you believe this is true?
3. Is Paul's command that Christians obey civil authority binding on us today?

CHAPTER 12

Free to Love, but Not Free Not to Love

ROM. 14:1 TO 15:13

PAUL now deals with a particular ethical problem related to the Christian's freedom from the law. There were some Christians in Rome who were not thoroughly convinced that in Christ they were totally free from the necessity of obeying all ceremonial or ritual laws. Some Christians, for example, believed that even though they were free in Christ, they were still not yet free to eat any food sold in the market or to treat all the seven days in the week as in every way alike. They apparently believed that they were still obliged to keep the Jewish Sabbath (Saturday) and that there were certain food laws that remained binding on them, which they could not totally disregard even though they were free from the law. As they felt subject to certain laws, they believed themselves to be guilty if they broke them. Paul calls such Christians the "weak" ones or those who are "weak in faith." In doing so he is not being derogatory or scornful, but he wishes to indicate by the term "weak" that these Christians are not yet able fully to appropriate the freedom they actually have in Christ. Those who act fully on their freedom, who like Paul himself are not afraid to be free and are not too timid to live fully in faith, Paul calls the "strong" ones. Let us now observe what Paul says about these two groups of Christians, the weak and the strong, both of whom were to be found in the church in Rome.

Paul begins by recognizing the fact that some people in the church believe they may eat everything, that in Christ they are free from all food laws. But others, the weak ones, believe that they may eat only vegetables. Paul tells the former to receive the latter without arguing with them about their legalism. Those who eat everything should not despise those who are still weak in faith and do not eat all things. The strong are always tempted to look down on the weak, to scorn them because of their weakness, but love does not permit this. The weak must be accepted by the strong in love, just as they are. They must not be pitied or despised but should be received as fellow believers.

And, on the other hand, those who abstain from eating certain foods should not stand in judgment over those who eat them. If the special temptation of the strong is scornfulness, the peculiar temptation of the weak is censoriousness. The people who, for religious reasons, eat only vegetables and not meat are apt to assume that their fellow Christians who do eat meat must be sinning against their conscience.

Therefore, the abstainer condemns as a sinner the one who eats. The fact is, however, that the ones who eat are more enlightened than the ones who abstain: their conscience is not afflicted by their eating; they are exercising the freedom they have in Christ and are not sinning when they eat. So the abstainers should not condemn those who eat, for *God* does not condemn them. The people who do not abstain are servants of Christ. They stand or fall in their relation to Christ and not in relation to their weak brethren.

Paul believed that the law had been responsible for creating estrangement among those under the law. Those who obeyed the law elevated themselves in their own eyes above those who did not obey, as the Pharisee in Jesus' parable thanked God that he was superior to the tax collector. And so the law brought division among people: it produced animosities and resentments, conceit and hatred. But those in Christ were free from the law, free from the code of prohibitions and commandments that had separated them from their neighbors. Therefore, they ought to have been freed from divisions that had been caused by the law.

But what was the situation in the Roman church? There were those who exercised their freedom in a radical way, who took with extreme seriousness their deliverance from the law. There were others who were not yet able to live totally in the freedom they had been given by God in Christ. They still had the feeling that they stood under law, at least under *some* laws, and they were trying to combine their freedom in Christ with their obligation to these laws. The two groups were producing a division in the church similar to the old divisions produced by the law. The new division was also caused by laws. It was made up, however, not of those who obeyed and those who did not obey, but of those who were freed from the law and those who felt obligated to obey certain laws. The result was the same—animosity and mutual estrangement. Both groups were prone to the same sin—the sin of boasting over their superiority, the strong scorning the weak and the weak censuring the strong. Freedom from the law was producing a division in the church similar to that in Judaism caused by subservience to the law. And Paul's word to the divided parties is: You must accept each other, in Christ, as you are.

Paul's sympathies are with the strong, who are exercising their full freedom in Christ. They are not abstaining from any foods for religious reasons; nor are they observing certain days as different from other days. The weak must welcome them, for, though the weak may not realize it, *God* has accepted them. The fact is that they are not abstaining precisely *because* God has accepted them and granted them the freedom on which they are acting. But the important thing is not *what* one does but *why* one does it. All should know in their own minds why they eat or why they abstain. If their reason for eating or abstaining is that this is what they understand the *Lord* to require, then they can do no other. One does not act as a Christian, in faith, if one acts because the *law* commands the action, but one does act as a Christian if one believes that *Christ* commands what one does. One may be misguided in one's understanding of what Christ commands, as Paul, in this case, believes the weak ones are. Nevertheless, the Christians must act on such enlightenment as they have in Christ and not on the opinions of others.

Paul reminds the church that no one lives unto himself.

He does not mean, as he is often taken to mean, that everyone is necessarily related to and dependent upon his fellow human beings. He means, rather, that every Christian—and he is talking here only about Christians, weak and strong—must do what he or she does for no other reason than that Christ commands it. We must live for Christ and not for ourselves. If both the weak and the strong, those who abstain and those who do not, take their positions "in Christ," then grounds for the superiority of one group over the other cannot exist. The strong cannot boast in their freedom, for they are free only because Christ has made them free. And the weak cannot boast in their abstentions, for they are abstaining, not out of their own power in obedience to the law, but by grace and obedience to Christ. If, however, the strong are not strong *in Christ,* and the weak are not weak *in Christ,* then both may boast and both are guilty, for everything that is not done out of faith is sin.

The fact is, however, that whether we eat or whether we abstain, we are the Lord's, both in life and in death. We shall all stand before the judgment seat of God and give an account of ourselves before the Judge of all the earth, who does no wrong. At that time our eating will not be relevant, nor will our abstaining. The question will be whether we will acknowledge this, whether we will be willing to disavow any claims to righteousness for having eaten or not eaten, whether we will be willing to accept the grace of God for nothing and the intercession of Jesus Christ on our behalf. How ridiculous it is, then, for the weak to condemn their brothers or sisters in Christ and for the strong to despise their brothers or sisters in Christ!

Each lives only by the grace of God; neither earns any merit by his or her ways; both stand together in Christ before God as the recipients of sheer grace.

Paul now has a special word to say to those who are fully exercising their freedom. He warns them not to place an obstacle or a stumbling block before their weaker sisters and brothers. Paul himself is persuaded, in the Lord, that the strong ones are the enlightened ones, that the weak misunderstand the nature of their freedom as well as the nature of the single command under which they stand as Christians. He says that nothing is unclean in itself. An act can be evil *in itself* only under a legal system that prescribes the behavior people will follow. But for the believer an act is evil only if it is not a manifestation of love, only if one's motive was not in the interest of one's neighbor's well-being. Thus the criterion by which the action of a Christian is judged is not *what* was done—when an act is good or evil *in itself*—but *why* it was done—when an act is good or evil according to the *reason* it was done. Hence only the one who acted is in a position to judge whether what he or she did was good or evil. If believers are convinced that a certain food is unclean, the food must remain unclean for them until such time as they change their opinion about it. No one can tell another what is wrong for him or her to do.

But as long as there are differences in conviction with regard to what is clean and what is unclean—what is right and what is wrong—for as long as such differences exist, a special word must be addressed to the strong, to those who are more enlightened in Christ. For the strong can cause grief and even harm to the weak. How do they do this? One who believes in and fully lives out one's freedom in Christ will very often offend a fellow Christian who is not yet fully convinced that in Christ he or she stands only under the law of love. And sometimes the strong will do more than offend. They may lead weaker sisters and brothers to do what their conscience does not allow, thus leading them to sin. To cause a weaker one to sin is to sin oneself, because it is not to walk in love.

Paul is consistent in his criterion: one is free *to love;* one is not free *not* to love. One is free, in Christ, to eat any food if, in eating it, one does not cause a weaker brother to stumble, that is, to eat what one's conscience does not permit one to eat. One's freedom in Christ is freedom from law, but it is not freedom so to act that one is permitted to lead one's fellow believer to sin. So Paul admonishes the strong not to exercise their freedom in such a way as to destroy a brother or sister for whom Christ died. Here the issue is not *what* one does but *how* what one does affects one's neighbor in Christ.

And this leads Paul to remind his readers of a matter he continually stresses: the obligation of every believer to work for the *building up* of the church. Christians should always act to strengthen one another in Christ, to establish and maintain peace in the household of faith. To injure a fellow Christian is to mar the work of God, and to cause a brother or sister to fall is to tear down what God has built up. Christians are to yield their right to eat whatever they please if the exercise of this right would cause injury to a sister or brother.

Those who are strong, who are enlightened with regard

to their freedom, are not so for their own benefit. One is
made free in Christ not in order to please oneself but in
order to please one's neighbor. The freedom given in
Christ is freedom to love and to build up the church. A
Christian is made free not to do as *he* or *she* pleases but to
do as *God* pleases. And it is God's will that the community
of those who believe be made strong in love. In mutual love
there is mutual fortification, and it is, therefore, in *mutual*
relationships, in relationships with *others* in love, that the
individual, made free to love, finds his or her life. Freedom
to be isolated is no freedom at all, except that it is freedom
to die. The Christian, in being made free, is made free to
love *in a community*. All things are *lawful* for him or her, but
not all things build up the community. Christians are free
from law, but they are not free from responsibility for their
sisters and brothers in Christ. Therefore in their freedom
they ought to renounce the freedom they have from the law
and choose to love their neighbors. Christian freedom is
freedom to love, freedom to be reconciled and to be united
to one's neighbor and to God. And the exercising of this
freedom, which is freedom to love, involves pleasing the
neighbor and not the self.

In this connection Paul refers to Christ, who in his freedom did not please himself but, instead, took upon himself
the injuries of others. Paul does not quote Christ's words
as laws, but he does point to Christ's life—especially his
crucifixion—as an example. Christians must choose the way
of renunciation on behalf of their sisters and brothers for
whom Christ died, and their patient endurance will become
the ground of their hope.

For Further Thought . . .

1. Does Paul believe that a Christian should renounce his or her freedom if to exercise freedom would hurt a fellow Christian?
2. Is the Christian expected to yield his or her own freedom in favor of the freedom of another?

CHAPTER 13

The Body of Christ Is One

PAUL ends his discussion of particular ethical issues in chaps. 12:1 to 15:13 with a benediction that brings to a close the main part of one of the most significant and influential letters ever written—a document pored over by the church for twenty centuries, one whose contents never grow old. The letter to Rome, however, does not end with this benediction. There are two matters yet to be taken up: the matter of Paul's visit to the church at Rome and a long list of greetings sent to members of that church.

Concerning his visit to Rome, Paul reminds the church there that by the grace of God he has been sent, as a minister of Christ Jesus, to *Gentiles.* He has acted as a priest for the gospel of God in order that he might present the Gentiles as an offering to God, with which offering God would be pleased. Paul had preached the gospel from Jerusalem north into Syria, west through Asia Minor, across the

Aegean Sea into Achaia and Macedonia, and north as far as Illyricum (modern Yugoslavia). He had not wanted to preach where someone else had preached before him, not desiring, as he said, to build on another person's foundation. But he did want to go to Rome. Someone else had founded the church there, to be sure, but Rome was a unique city, the capital of the enormous empire called "Roman." Paul had wanted to visit the church there for many years but had repeatedly been prevented from doing so. Now, however, the time seemed ripe. He would pass through Rome on his way to Spain. He would not stay long in the city—not long enough to build on a foundation laid by someone else—but he would meet the church there, and, no doubt, preach to it. Then he would be sped on his way to far-off Spain.

But before Paul visited Rome on his trip west, he had first to go back to Jerusalem with the offering he had collected from Christians in Macedonia and Achaia. The Jerusalem church was poor, and Paul had told James, the Lord's brother, and other leaders of the church that he would raise money for them from among the Gentile churches. And now that the money had been collected, Paul wanted to take it to Jerusalem himself, even though in doing so he risked his life. Why didn't Paul send the offering back in the care of one of his trusted helpers? If he had done so, he could have saved a great deal of travel time and much energy, and he could much sooner have made his trip to Spain. Furthermore, he could have avoided the physical harm that he anticipated in Jerusalem. The reason he insisted on taking the offering personally is probably that in this way he could demonstrate, by means of such a significant act, the unity of the church.

Paul had had differences with the Jerusalem church. He had not been willing to alter his gospel in the light of these differences, but neither would he consent to a divided church. There could be differences of opinion, but there could be only one church. The body of Christ was one body, and it could not function if one part were severed from another. So by going to Jerusalem with an offering collected from Gentile Christians in far-off Europe, Paul could show that he, and the Jerusalem Christians, and the Gentile Christians of lands far away constituted one church. The world was divided into provinces and empires, and its peoples were separated by race and religion and tongue, but there is only one church—"one Lord, one faith, one baptism, one God and Father of us all."

So Paul took the offering, and the book of Acts records his narrow escape with his life, his arrest, his trial, and finally his trip to Rome for a hearing. Was Paul released from his Roman imprisonment and did he ever get to Spain? The answer to these questions is still shrouded among the secrets of history.

Tacked on, so to speak, to the end of Romans is a long list of greetings that Paul sent to Christians whom he knew there. Among these are Aquila and his wife Prisca, about whom we hear in Acts; Epaenetus, who was the first convert in the province of Asia in Asia Minor; Andronicus and Junias, who were Christians before Paul and whom Paul refers to as "apostles"; and a deacon named Phoebe, who came from the church at Cenchreae, near Corinth.

At the end of the greetings is a warning to watch out for and to avoid those who create dissensions and undermine what the church has been taught. These people were clever and could quite easily deceive unsuspecting, simple folk.

Finally, we learn that Paul dictated his letter to one by the name of Tertius, who had done the actual writing. And at the end, what we should expect from Paul—an ascription of glory forever and ever, "to the only wise God . . . through Jesus Christ! Amen."

For Further Thought . . .

Was the offering for the poor at Jerusalem important to Paul? If so, why? Note what he says about it in Rom. 15:25–32; Gal. 2:10; 1 Cor. 16:1–4; 2 Cor. chaps. 8–9.